PENGUIN (P) CLASSICS

THE IMITATION OF CHRIST

THOMAS À KEMPIS was born at Kempen in 1379/80. By this time, the Sisters of Common Life had been established by Geert Grote (1340–84), founder of the Modern Devout. At the age of thirteen, Thomas visited his elder brother John who had joined the monastic branch of the movement, the Augustinian community at Windesheim. John persuaded Thomas to reside in Deventer with the Brothers of Common Life, who were supervised and had been founded by Thomas' key mentor Florens Radewijns. In 1399 Radewijns allowed him to travel to Zwolle to seek admission to the new monastery at Mount St Agnes, where his brother had become Prior. He was professed in 1407 and was ordained a priest in 1413/14. Thomas wrote many other devotional works besides *The Imitation of Christ*, his masterpiece, and several biographies including those of Grote and Radewijns; indeed his long life was devoted to the study of the Scriptures and the Early Fathers. In 1425 he was elected Sub-Prior for the first time, acted as the Master of the Novices and kept the monastery's Chronicle. He died in 1471.

The Very Revd ROBERT JEFFERY was born in 1935 and ordained in 1959. He has written on matters of Church history, spirituality, mission and ecumenism. In 1978 he became Archdeacon of Salop, and was Dean of Worcester 1987–96 and subsequently Canon and Sub-Dean of Christ Church, Oxford. He retired in 2002 and is an Honorary Doctor of Divinity of Birmingham University.

MAX VON HABSBURG was educated at Ampleforth College and at the University of St Andrews, where he took an M.A. in Modern History and completed an M.Litt. and Ph.D. in the Reformation Studies Institute. Since 2001 he has taught in the History Department at Oundle School, Northamptonshire. His latest book is *Catholic and Protestant Translations of the Imitatio Christi, 1425–1650: From Late Medieval Classic to Early Modern Bestseller* (Farnham: Ashgate, 2011).

THOMAS À KEMPIS

The Imitation of Christ

Translated and with Notes by
ROBERT JEFFERY

with an Introduction by
MAX VON HABSBURG

PENGUIN BOOKS

PENGUIN CLASSICS

Published by the Penguin Group
Penguin Books Ltd, 80 Strand, London WC2R ORL, England
Penguin Group (USA) Inc., 375 Hudson Street, New York, New York 10014, USA
Penguin Group (Canada), 90 Eglinton Avenue East, Suite 700, Toronto, Ontario, Canada M4P 2Y3
(a division of Pearson Penguin Canada Inc.)
Penguin Ireland, 25 St Stephen's Green, Dublin 2, Ireland (a division of Penguin Books Ltd)
Penguin Group (Australia), 707 Collins Street, Melbourne, Victoria 3008, Australia
(a division of Pearson Australia Group Pty Ltd)
Penguin Books India Pvt Ltd, 11 Community Centre, Panchsheel Park, New Delhi – 110 017, India
Penguin Group (NZ), 67 Apollo Drive, Rosedale, Auckland 0632, New Zealand
(a division of Pearson New Zealand Ltd)
Penguin Books (South Africa) (Pty) Ltd, Block D, Rosebank Office Park,
181 Jan Smuts Avenue, Parktown North, Gauteng 2193, South Africa

Penguin Books Ltd, Registered Offices: 80 Strand, London WC2R ORL, England

www.penguin.com

This translation first published in Great Britain by Penguin Classics 2013
003

Translation and editorial material copyright © Robert Jeffery, 2013
Introduction copyright © Max von Habsburg, 2013
All rights reserved

The moral right of the authors of the editorial material and the translator has been asserted

Direct Scripture quotations contained herein are from the New Revised Standard Version
Bible copyright © 1989 by the Division of Christian Education of the National Council of
Churches of Christ in the USA and are used by permission. All rights reserved.

Set in 10.25/12.25pt PostScript Adobe Sabon
Typeset by Jouve (UK), Milton Keynes
Printed in Great Britain by Clays Ltd, St Ives plc

ISBN: 978-0-141-19176-8

www.greenpenguin.co.uk

MIX
Paper from
responsible sources
FSC
www.fsc.org   FSC™ C018179

Penguin Books is committed to a sustainable
future for our business, our readers and our planet.
This book is made from Forest Stewardship
Council™ certified paper.

ALWAYS LEARNING   **PEARSON**

Contents

THE IMITATION

OF CHRIST

Part One:
The Chapters of Book One

Part Two:
The Chapters of Book Two

Part Three:
The Chapters of Book Four

Part Four:
The Chapters of Book Three

Chronology

1340 Geert Grote born in Deventer

1365 John à Kempis (Thomas' brother) born

1374 Sisters of Common Life established by Grote

1379/80 Thomas à Kempis (known as Haemmerlein or Hemerken) born in Kempen

1384 Grote dies; first house of Brothers of Common Life established at Zwolle

1387 Florens Radewijns (*c.*1350–1400) founds monastery at Windesheim

*c.*1392–9 Thomas à Kempis visits Windesheim; his brother sends him (with a letter of introduction) to Radewijns in Deventer, where he lives with the Brothers of Common Life and attends the chapter school of St Lebuin

1395 Windesheim Congregation founded (*Constitutions* approved by Pope Boniface IX), including communities at Marienborn, Nieuwlicht, Eemstein and Windesheim

1398 Foundation of monastery at Mount St Agnes, near Zwolle

*c.*1399 Thomas moves to Zwolle, yet the date of his arrival at Mount St Agnes is uncertain

*c.*1400 First convent established at Diepenveen (founded by Salome Sticken and John Brinckerinck)

1406 Thomas becomes a novice at Mount St Agnes

1407 Thomas' solemn profession of vows; there are now twelve monasteries in the Windesheim Congregation

1413/14 Thomas ordained priest

1424 Earliest dated manuscript of Book One of the *Imitatio Christi*

1427 Earliest dated manuscript of all four books of the *Imitatio Christi*

1425–c.31 Thomas elected Sub-Prior (for the first time) at Mount St Agnes

1429–31 Mount St Agnes community chooses to live in exile rather than disobey a papal interdict imposed on the diocese of Utrecht

1431 Thomas stays with his brother near Arnhem

1432 John à Kempis dies

1441 Date of autograph manuscript

1448–58 Re-elected Sub-Prior at Mount St Agnes

1471 Thomas à Kempis dies

*c.***1471** First (Latin) edition of the *Imitatio*, printed in Augsburg

1511 *Devotio moderna* consists of eighty-four monasteries and thirteen convents

Introduction

If a man tells you that he is fond of the *Imitation*, view him
with sudden suspicion; he is either a dabbler or a saint . . .
Heaven help us if we find easy reading in the *Imitation of
Christ*.[1]

Ronald Knox

The *Imitatio Christi*, commonly attributed to Thomas à Kempis,
is a classic of Western spirituality with an extraordinary pub-
lishing history. The *Imitatio* encapsulates the fundamental
tenets of Christian devotion: its inherent Biblicism; its Christ-
centred focus; and its exposition of the main Christian virtues
of humility, redemptive self-denial and grace.[2] There were over
900 manuscripts of the *Imitatio* produced between 1420 and
1500; it appeared in Middle Dutch as early as it did in Latin,
and it was quickly translated into the major European languages. While the use of Latin allowed the *Imitatio* to cross
geographical and linguistic boundaries, the existence of three
different manuscript versions in England illustrates that Latin
did not necessarily standardize texts.[3] The *Imitatio*'s transition
from ubiquitous manuscript to early printed bestseller was
seamless: there are over 100 extant incunabula (editions that
were printed, rather than handwritten) before 1500. Günther
Zainer printed the first edition of the *Imitatio* c.1471 on a
Benedictine press in Augsburg. William Caxton's successors,
Richard Pynson (1448–1528) and Wynkyn de Worde (d. 1534),
collaborated with the English Bridgettines and Carthusians and
printed the first English editions of the *Imitatio*.[4]

Between 1500 and 1650, over 650 editions of the *Imitatio*
were printed in a wide array of languages including Arabic,
Armenian, Chinese, Czech, Hungarian, Japanese, Polish and
Ukrainian.[5] A very broad range of individuals adopted the

Imitatio during the Early and Late Modern periods including St Thomas More, Caspar Schwenckfeld, St Ignatius of Loyola, St Teresa of Avila, Johann Arndt, John Wesley, Samuel Johnson,[6] Thomas Keble, George Eliot, Pope John XXIII, Dietrich Bonhoeffer and Thomas Merton.

Thomas Carlyle acknowledged the extent to which the *Imitatio* was embraced by a wide range of Christian communities. He sent a copy to his mother on 13 February 1833, in which he inscribed the following words: 'None, I believe, except the Bible, has been so universally read and loved by Christians of all tongues and sects.' Peter Burke has affirmed that, other than the Bible, no work was reproduced or translated more frequently, while John Van Engen has described it as undoubtedly the 'most influential devotional book in Western Christian history'.[7] The Indian Hindu monk Swami Vivekananda (1863–1902) and the spiritual teacher Eknath Easwaran (1910–99) bear testimony to the *Imitatio*'s appeal beyond Christian circles.[8]

Not initially conceived as a single work, the *Imitatio Christi* consists of four distinct books which were eventually transcribed together due to their thematic similarities. Earliest copies rarely included all four books and the title *De Imitatione Christi* is taken from the first words of Book One. The earliest manuscript of Book One dates back to 1424, with all four books represented in a manuscript dated three years later.[9] The autograph manuscript of 1441 lists them in the same order as this translation: advice helpful to the spiritual life; advice on living the inner life; devout encouragement to receive Holy Communion; the Book of Inner Consolation. The final two books are set out in the form of a dialogue between Christ and His disciple. Many manuscripts and printed editions place the book on Holy Communion at the end, which explains why it is usually designated as the fourth book. Although all four books were probably composed by the same author, the *Imitatio* generally lacks a systematic linear structure.[10]

AUTHORSHIP DEBATE

There are over forty claimants to the authorship, including Geert Grote, founder of the *devotio moderna* (Modern Devout), the religious movement from which the *Imitatio* emerged.[11] Different manuscripts and early printed editions referred either to Thomas à Kempis, Augustinian canon of the Windesheim Congregation, Jean Gerson (1363–1429), Chancellor of the University of Paris, St Bernard of Clairvaux (1090–1153), Ludolph of Saxony (*c.*1300–78), or Giovanni Gersen (Benedictine Abbot of Vercelli, 1220–40), or else the work was left anonymous. Although Kempis seems to be the strongest claimant, his authorship is not beyond doubt. Gerson appears to be Kempis' most credible challenger; numerous manuscripts and incunabula were assigned to him.[12] Yet it is surely revealing that Gerson's brother did not attribute the *Imitatio* to him when he collated his works. Numerous contemporary witnesses (albeit with strong links to Kempis' circles) supported Kempis' claim. The Jesuits, who contributed more to the *Imitatio*'s early printed circulation than any other organization, spoke fondly of the 'little Gerson' but later transferred their allegiance to Kempis. The interest in the authorship debate persisted in later centuries, focusing on Gersen, the Benedictine claimant, and Kempis, the latter supported by Jesuits and Augustinians. Nineteenth- and twentieth-century research on the *Imitatio* also focused mainly on the identity of its author, without reaching a definitive answer. The current consensus is that the *Imitatio* definitely originated in the communities of the *devotio moderna*. This Introduction assumes that Kempis was its author.

The doubts raised about Kempis' authorship are pertinent to the *Imitatio*'s spirituality and that of the Modern Devout. Most works originating from the *devotio moderna* were anonymous: claiming authorship could hinder the pursuit of humility, and originality was rarely a primary consideration. The blurred distinction between author and copyist was reinforced by the nature of the *devotio moderna*'s spiritual note-taking (*rapiaria*). Writers tended to record important passages from spiritual texts without attribution. Nikolaus Staubach has contended that the hybrid nature of the *Imitatio*'s *rapiaria* may be why Kempis was reluctant to claim authorship. This may also explain the ambiguity that surrounds the colophon of the autograph manuscript copy of 1441, which ends with the following words: 'Finished and completed in the year of our Lord 1441 by the hand of brother Thomas à Kempis at Mount St Agnes near Zwolle' (Royal Library, Brussels). It is unclear whether Kempis wrote this as author and/or copyist.[13] Given the uncertainty about the *Imitatio*'s author, it is more valuable to set Kempis within the broader context of the *devotio moderna* than to trace his life in detail. If Kempis did not write the work, then one of his contemporaries (associated with the different branches of the movement) did.

THE *IMITATIO*, THOMAS À KEMPIS AND THE *DEVOTIO MODERNA*

The *Imitatio*'s success has been credited to the text's universality. Johan Huizinga was not alone in attributing the *Imitatio*'s popularity to its apparent transcendence of cultural boundaries, yet the timeless characteristics of its spirituality only partly explain its widespread circulation.[14] The *Imitatio* must be placed within its proper context, namely the circles of the *devotio moderna*. This is similarly true for subsequent editions and translations, particularly since the practice of translation was invariably dictated by the broader social, cultural and (from 1520 onwards) theological context.

The *Imitatio* was the manifesto for the *devotio moderna*, a movement consisting of Brothers and Sisters of Common Life (religious communities without vows) and cloistered Augustinian canons and canonesses.[15] The movement's founder, Geert Grote, established the Sisters of Common Life in 1374. Five years later, Florens Radewijns founded the Brothers of Common Life and this was followed in 1387 by the foundation of the Augustinian canons at Windesheim. Manuscript-copying was integral to all components of the Modern Devout and was considered a 'good work' and spiritually uplifting. It provided income as well as religious books to read, and allowed the movement to defend its *medius status* (representing their existence between the monastery and the world) and their use of the vernacular. The Modern Devout responded to the marked increase in book production by establishing libraries and compiling detailed reading lists. The *Imitatio* obviously benefited from the *devotio moderna*'s remarkable expansion: eighty-two Brothers of Common Life houses by 1470; ninety Sisters of Common Life communities by 1500; and 100 monasteries by 1511.

The *devotio moderna*'s monastic branch helped to mould the *Imitatio*'s spirituality, though numerous scholars have mistakenly asserted that it was written exclusively for monks.[16] Although Grote had personally rejected monasticism, he undertook a lengthy retreat at a Carthusian monastery (Munnikhuizen) and shared Johannes Busch's view that monasticism represented a more perfect form of religious life. At the community of Mount St Agnes, Kempis became steeped in monasticism, and as Sub-Prior and Novice Master he contributed personally to the formation of novices.[17] Although monastic vows are not mentioned explicitly in the *Imitatio*, the text's spirituality is particularly suited to the cloister.[18] Evidence clearly shows that it was widely circulated within the male and female communities of the Windesheim Congregation.[19] This was particularly the case in the later 1400s as the *devotio moderna* underwent a process of monasticization, partly stemming from the mounting opposition to the fact that the Brethren of Common Life had no vows.

Nevertheless, the contents of the *Imitatio* and diverse nature of the *devotio moderna* reveal that the text was not written solely for monks. From the very beginning, the *Imitatio* addressed the Modern Devout and laity who were not cloistered. The monastery at Windesheim was founded in 1387, three years after Grote's death, by which time he had already established the Sisters of Common Life. He defended their right, and later that of the Brothers, to pursue a religious life without the profession of vows. Emphasis was placed on a communal life in the world, modelled on the New Testament and the early Church. The Brethren's active and contemplative lives closely resembled those of their monastic contemporaries: book-copying and book-binding; liturgical participation; spiritual note-taking and meditative prayer.

Kempis' formative experiences with the Brethren in Deventer (and later Zwolle) during the 1390s (under his mentor Radewijns) ensured that he was also sensitive to their traditions and spirituality. Patience, humility and silence, the virtues espoused in the *Imitatio*, were equally pertinent to those living in the outside world. The *Imitatio* called for withdrawal from worldly values; this did not necessitate embarking on a monastic career. Exemplary monks, notably the Carthusians, were celebrated more for their dedication and perseverance than their cloistered existence. The *Imitatio* was embraced by the laity, especially the schoolboys housed by the Brothers. Although the Brothers seldom taught boys, they acted as their spiritual directors. While Grote remained in the world and Kempis eventually joined the Windesheim canons, both advocated the lay readership of vernacular devotional literature. With that broad context in mind, the *Imitatio* deliberately accommodated the movement's different components from the outset.

THE *IMITATIO*'S SPIRITUALITY

Biblicism

Noted for its Biblicism, the *Imitatio*'s ideas often appear only to be adaptations of biblical texts.[20] Kempis copied two complete Bibles in his lifetime; he had an intimate knowledge of the Bible and that familiarity with the Scriptures was consistent with the *devotio moderna*'s practices. The Bible provided the main source for spiritual reading, collations (talks for spiritual edification) and sermons delivered within their communities. From a spiritual perspective, biblical knowledge was considered pointless without practical application. As we are reminded in Book One, 'If you knew the whole Bible by heart and the teachings of all the philosophers, what good would that be without the grace and love of God?'[21] This also provides a particular interpretation of learning and its relative value.

Learning

Theological speculation could work to the detriment of devotion. As Kempis warned, 'What use is it for learned people to discuss the doctrine of the Trinity if they have no humility, and so displease the Trinity? Learned words do not make anyone wise or holy; it is a good life which draws us closer to God. I would rather feel deep sorrow than be able to define it.'[22] A believer with no formal academic training (like Gerard Zerbolt, 1367–98) was not at a spiritual disadvantage in the face of a scholar (like Geert Grote). This is a key strand of the *Imitatio's* spirituality: 'A humble peasant, who serves God, is more pleasing to God than a conceited intellectual, who knows the course of the stars but ignores the things of the spirit.'[23]

The *devotio moderna* (including Kempis) were not known for their theological prowess. They professed a preference for books of piety rather than academic tomes, though learning was not to be neglected altogether. The *Imitatio's* perspective suited the varying capabilities of the Modern Devout and their followers (notably those schools with which the *devotio moderna* had links). In the final reckoning, readers would be judged according to their piety, not their intellect.[24]

Interiority

Inward forms of spirituality are integral to all four books. The *Imitatio* prescribes that outward actions should be governed by inward thoughts. Similarly, books, images or statues presented a point of departure for higher forms of contemplation. The *Imitatio's* spirituality was responding to the prevalence, not the absence, of religious objects. This was certainly true of the *devotio moderna*, under whose supervision churches were decorated and books were illuminated. The strong sense of interiority does not mean that outward forms of devotion were insignificant: as Kempis remarked in Book One, 'There should be a careful scrutiny and organization of both our inward and outward life, since both are essential to our growth.'[25]

Contrition and Suffering

The stress on interiority is reinforced by the constant need to profess sorrow for sin. The infrequency of formal confession partly explains why so much emphasis was placed on contrition. The *devotio moderna* established a chapter of faults to allow for more rigorous self-examination. Readers were given stark reminders of their own frailties: 'Today you confess your sins; tomorrow you again commit the very sins you have confessed!'[26] The understanding of contrition is also given a liturgical setting: 'Deep sorrow for sin is an acceptable sacrifice to You, Lord, and is more fragrant in Your sight than clouds of incense.'[27] The need to be contrite was reinforced by the poignant reminder of Christ's Passion. Believers were expected to endure the trials of this earthly life. As Kempis wrote in Book One, 'if you make no provision for your own soul, who will care for you in the future? The present moment is very precious. Now is the hour of favour; now is the day of salvation.'[28] Kempis believed in purgatory, Masses for the dead and intercessory prayers, though the *Imitatio*'s preoccupation lay with what could be done in the present. Believers were to be consoled by the redemptive significance of suffering.[29]

Christ and Mary

The *Imitatio* invoked its readers to follow Christ. Instead of presenting actual moments from Christ's life, the *Imitatio* dwelt on His virtues and humanity.[30] Devotion to Christ was considered to be a stepping-stone to more profound contemplation: 'If it is hard to contemplate high and heavenly things, take rest in the Passion of Christ, and love to hide in His sacred wounds.'[31] Van Engen has argued that the attention to Christ in Kempis' works was so marked that 'there was in effect, if not necessarily in conscious intention, something of a shift toward a more exclusively Christocentric form of piety'.[32] While Christ predominates in the *Imitatio* (Books Three and Four include dialogues between Christ and His disciple), the Virgin Mary is only mentioned once.[33] The lack of references to Marian devotion in the *Imitatio* is not representative of the *devotio moderna* as a whole. The first chapel and altar of Mount St Agnes were consecrated in honour of Mary; the first house of the Sisters of Common Life and the first convent also chose Mary as their patroness.

The Saints

Christ served as the model for devotion to the saints, which is strongly advocated in the *Imitatio*: 'And anyone who speaks lightly of any of the Saints, speaks lightly both of Myself and of all the company of heaven.'[34] The *Imitatio*'s interpretation of Christian exemplars is rooted in the *devotio moderna*'s affinity for the Desert Fathers.[35] Rather than dwelling on the affection for individual saints, the *Imitatio* drew attention to the virtues which they extolled (their humility and self-denial; some suffered to the point of death).[36] As Christ insists in Book Three, 'Do not argue over the merits of the Saints, which is the holiest, or which the greater in the Kingdom of Heaven . . . It is better to pray to the Saints with devout prayer and sorrow, and to implore their glorious prayers, than to search into their secrets with pointless curiosity.'[37] Readers were discouraged from dwelling on the saints' miracles, a theme replicated in the *devotio moderna*'s numerous *Vitae* (biographies written to edify their own members).[38] Interestingly, the Windesheim Congregation reformed their liturgical calendar, reducing the number of saints' and feast days.[39]

Mass

Book Four (devout encouragement to receive Holy Communion) focuses on Eucharistic devotion and implies that the *Imitatio*'s overall purpose is to prepare believers to receive the Body of Christ. Interior preparation included sacramental confession: 'I am so prone to frequent lapses and so quickly grow lukewarm and careless, that it is essential that I renew, cleanse and activate myself by frequent prayer and confession, and by the reception of Your Body.'[40] The insistence on reverence was typified by silent contemplation, rather than an emphasis on outward (physical or verbal) gestures. The

Imitatio's interiority was partly a response to the visual components of Eucharistic piety that had led to the establishment of the Feast of Corpus Christi in 1264. The *Imitatio*'s spirituality sought to shift the excessive importance attached to the external manifestations of devotion to inward contemplation. Careful spiritual preparation was a prerequisite for the sacramental reception of the Body of Christ. Where sacramental participation was not possible, spiritual communion was recommended. The book also emphasized the dignity of the priestly office and how celebrants of the Eucharist were expected to lead exemplary lives.[41] Book Four is not solely directed at priests, though there is a strong emphasis on priestly responsibilities.[42] Not all manuscript copies and printed editions of the *Imitatio* included Book Four.

THE *IMITATIO* IN THE EARLY
MODERN WORLD[43]

The First Jesuits

The numerous editions of the *Imitatio* owe a considerable debt to the Society of Jesus, one of the Early Modern period's most influential organizations.[44] The Jesuit Order's impressive growth greatly contributed to the *Imitatio*'s circulation.[45] Ignatius of Loyola, who founded the Jesuits, recommended it frequently and when he was General of the Society he had only two books permanently on his desk: the New Testament and the *Imitatio*. Jesuit adoption of the *Imitatio* largely stemmed from Ignatius' recommendation in the *Spiritual Exercises*. They deliberately chose a well-established text that was consistent with their spirituality. Jesuits subsequently produced Latin editions, many of which were then translated into European and non-European languages. They also revised the translations of non-Jesuits, often commissioning printers and even establishing their own presses. The *Imitatio* was recommended reading within the Jesuit houses, notably in the rules for the Master of Novices, first printed in 1580 under the Jesuit General Everard Mercurian. The appearance of Jesuit-sponsored Latin editions in the seventeenth century may have been triggered by the Antwerp Jesuit College's inheriting in 1595 of an original autograph manuscript of the *Imitatio*.[46] This may also explain why in the 1600s the Jesuits identified Kempis as the author.

The Jesuit association with the *Imitatio* appears to sit uncomfortably with some recent Jesuits. For many Catholics (not just Jesuits), the *Imitatio*'s contempt for the world seems outdated and inappropriate. The *Imitatio*'s 'pessimistic' view of human nature has been contrasted with the more positive interpretation presented at the Second Vatican Council, especially in the document entitled *Gaudium et Spes*.[47] Consequently, leading Jesuit scholars have chosen to emphasize and magnify the discrepancies between the *Imitatio*'s spirituality and that of the early Jesuits. Joseph de Guibert claimed that:

> Ignatius' thought about the apostolic service of God and about labour throughout the world for the salvation of souls is something almost entirely foreign to the *Imitatio*. Also, the tendency towards withdrawing oneself from the world, both in affection and also in fact, and the praise given to the retired life within a cell – all this transports us in the *Imitatio* into an order of thought far removed from that of Ignatius.[48]

These apparent discrepancies should not disguise the fact that the *Imitatio* was widely read in Early Modern Jesuit circles. The evidence that the *Imitatio* was a key devotional text among the early Jesuits is unambiguous, a historical reality that twentieth-century debates within the Roman Catholic Church cannot alter.

Protestant adoption of the Imitatio

Although Martin Luther is known to have praised the piety of the Brethren of Common Life, there is no evidence that he was familiar with the *Imitatio* and he is unlikely to have held it in high regard. After all, it retained references to purgatory and intercessory prayers to the saints, which Lutheran theology denied. The notion of *imitatio Christi* seemed to support the value of meritorious works, which Luther's central doctrine, justification by faith alone (*sola fide*), had rendered obsolete. The interior reform promoted by the *Imitatio* was closely intertwined with preparation for the Mass. Protestants rejected Catholic Eucharistic theology and the mediatory powers of priests. These factors explain why early Protestant reformers distanced themselves from the *Imitatio*.[49]

Despite this, some Protestants were attracted to the *Imitatio*'s Christocentricity. Christ's words in Book Three can be interpreted theologically as well as spiritually: 'Apart from Me, there can be no help, no good advice and no lasting cure.'[50] This was reinforced by the text's interiority and by its well-established accessibility to the laity. The *Imitatio*'s pessimistic view of human nature, characterized by the juxtaposition of Nature and Grace in Book Three, appeared to satisfy even a Protestant theological framework: 'So the nature which You created good and upright has now become the total expression of corruption and weakness; for when it is left to itself it turns always towards evil and low things.'[51] The lack of any references to the Sacraments (excluding Book Four) was most convenient. Protestants appreciated that the *Imitatio* favoured the subordination of external forms of religion to inner piety – for example, its sceptical view of pilgrimages and relics.

The *Imitatio*'s biblical roots were an obvious point of attraction; Protestants regarded the Bible as the sole source of authority (*Sola Scriptura*). The centrepiece of the Reformation was to make the vernacular Bible widely available. The *Imitatio* advocated reading of the Bible and its magnetism was largely due to its inherent Biblicism. The existence of a devotional text alongside the Bible went to the heart of Protestant theology; by expounding the Scriptures, Protestants could be inspired to lead a life of greater religious fervour. The Bible crucially provided translators with a theological filter through which any non-biblical accretions on doctrine and practice could be erased. The goal of Protestant translators and editors was not to replicate the true sense of Kempis' original text; anything which did not conform to the Protestant interpretation of the Bible was removed. In addition to the notable absence of Book Four, Early Modern Protestant translations omitted any references to monasticism, intercessory prayers to the saints and purgatory.

The sections retained by Protestants are also worthy of mention. While references to purgatory were omitted, the quintessential purgatorial experience in the *Imitatio* was suffering on earth, a viewpoint which Protestants and Catholics shared. The majority of references to merit relate to Christ, rather than any intrinsic righteousness emanating from believers themselves. The disciple testifies to this in Book Three: 'I, who am Your servant, possess nothing that is not Your gift and I have no merit of my own. All things are Yours, both what You have given and what You have created.'[52] It is striking how little editing was required in numerous chapters of the *Imitatio*. The Protestantization of the text is characterized by the removal of a portion of its Catholic elements; with few significant additions, the process of translation did not render the final version Protestant *per se*. When studied in isolation, Protestant translations of the *Imitatio* do not appear to be Protestant in doctrinal terms. That some Protestant editions have provenances from Jesuit colleges might suggest that even the Jesuits did not recognize the Protestant authorship of the translation. There does not appear to be any reason why Jesuits could not derive immense spiritual profit from a Protestant translation, regardless of the Protestant filter adopted in the translation process.

With Lutherans preoccupied with theological controversies, there were no Protestant editions of the *Imitatio* in the first decade of the Reformation. However, as time progressed, a number of Protestants translated the *Imitatio*: the Silesian reformer and spiritualist Caspar Schwenckfeld (1489–1561); the Swiss reformer Leo Jud (1482–1542); Sebastian Castellio (1515–63), educational reformer, biblical scholar and leading advocate of religious toleration; two figures from the mainstream of the Elizabeth Settlement, Edward Hake (fl.1564–1604) and Thomas Rogers (c.1553–1616); and one of the leading proponents of early German Pietism, Johann Arndt (1555–1621).[53] The likes of Schwenckfeld, Castellio (and the Anabaptists and Familists who read the text) distrusted the notion of a visible Church.[54]

The *Imitatio*'s interiority and the absence of a sacramental framework (without Book Four) attracted spiritualists like Schwenckfeld, who held the externals of faith in contempt. In contrast, Hake and Rogers adopted the *Imitatio* as part of an attempt to strengthen their notion of a visible Church, one that was threatened from numerous sides (Puritans, Crypto-Catholics, Recusants, Jesuits, Anabaptists and Familists), all of whom, as it happens, found the *Imitatio* appealing.

In the seventeenth century, representatives of the opposing factions of Puritanism and Arminianism were also attracted to the text and appropriated or promoted it, as did some Church of Scotland clerics.[55] Seventeenth-century translators included John Preston, who was associated with the 'hotter sort of Protestants'; and, in contrast, the Arminian William Page, who wrote in his 1639 translation of the *Imitatio* that the different churches (Catholic and Protestant) should call for unity and undertake a crusade against the Turks. Even William Shakespeare seems to have drawn on the *Imitatio* in the speeches of Friar Laurence in *Romeo and Juliet* and of the exiled Duke in *As You Like It*.[56]

LATE MODERN ADVOCATES
OF THE *IMITATIO*

The popularity of the *Imitatio* is undiminished in the modern age. Within Catholic circles, in addition to continued interest and appreciation among the Jesuits, the *Imitatio* was adopted by a succession of influential figures from the 1700s onwards.[57] These included Richard Challoner, one of the eighteenth century's leading English Roman Catholics, who produced an edition of the *Imitatio*.[58] The *Imitatio* was also advocated by St Thérèse of Lisieux (1873–97), Pope John XXIII (1881–1963), Thomas Merton (1915–68), the Anglo-American writer and mystic, and Edith Cavell (1865–1915), who read it on a daily basis. The historian Lord Acton described the *Imitatio* as 'the most perfectly normal expression of Catholic thought, as it bears the least qualifying impress of time and place'.[59] Acton's fondness for the *Imitatio* was attributed to the 'touch of late-medieval resignation reflected in neo-Gothic nostalgia of nineteenth-century Catholicism'.[60] Ronald Knox (1888–1957), English priest and theologian, later undertook his own (albeit incomplete) translation of the *Imitatio*; his words are quoted at the beginning of this Introduction.

The *Imitatio* also thrived in a variety of Late Modern English Protestant circles, and numerous editions were published under Anglican auspices. Unsurprisingly, but significantly, the *Imitatio* found favour with adherents of the Oxford Movement, and was translated by Thomas Keble (1793–1875).[61] Driven by the ideal of restoring the High Church of the seventeenth century, the principles of the nineteenth-century Oxford Movement retained some Catholic sympathies, rendering the adoption of the *Imitatio* less challenging.

At the other end of the spectrum, the *Imitatio* was well received by the Quakers, a striking fact given their rejection of the Sacraments. Quakers considered the 'inner light' to be superior to the Bible and the Church. This has strong parallels with Schwenckfeld and the spiritualist tradition, which formed an important background for the *Imitatio*'s early Protestant appropriation.[62] Founded in 1668 and granted greater freedom via the Toleration Act (1689), the Quakers may even have benefited from their association with such an established and highly regarded text.

The *Imitatio* was a key spiritual work for the leading advocate and founder of Methodism, John Wesley (1703–91). One of the earliest entries in Wesley's private diary, in 1726, alludes to his providential discovery of the *Imitatio*, which he later identified and published as *The Christian's Pattern*. His appreciation for the text was reiterated in his *Plain Account of Christian Perfection*, the most elaborate summary of his spirituality. As he himself stated, 'The nature and extent of Inward Religion, the religion of the heart, now appeared to me in a stronger light than ever it had done before.'[63]

However, Wesley also expressed his anger at Kempis for being 'too strict', even though initially he read him only in George Stanhope's late-seventeenth-century translation. These criticisms largely explain the amendments and omissions in Wesley's revised and abridged version of his own translation.[64] Making only a few minor changes to Book Two, Wesley removed five chapters from Book One, the majority being references to religious communities.[65] Wesley's High Church beliefs regarding frequent Communion and the Real Presence account for the few changes to Book Four on Holy Communion, with only three chapters left out. Most conspicuous of all is Wesley's removal of over fifteen chapters from Book Three. The recurrent themes within those sections include the weakness of human nature, the worthlessness of human help, the lack of security from temptation, the bitterness of life and the need to be dead and crucified to the world.[66] These themes define Kempis' strictness, which so angered Wesley. After all, Wesley rejected predestination and his 'mature doctrine of salvation shifted away from the Reformation's stress on justification and towards the development of a holy life'.[67] Wesley's positive appreciation reflects a significant shift away from earlier Protestant distaste for the *Imitatio*.

The *Imitatio* was promoted by a number of writers and academics, as well as by clerical members of respective Christian denominations. The lexicographer Dr Samuel Johnson (1709–84), the ecclesiastical historian Charles Bigg (1840–1908), the writer and printer Samuel Richardson (1689–1761) and the Irish writers James Joyce (1882–1941) and William Naughton (1910–92) all professed an interest in the *Imitatio*. Such was his enthusiasm for the text that Naughton's house in Ballasalla was called Kempis. Auguste Comte (1798–1857), the founder of positive philosophy, described the *Imitatio* as the 'inextinguishable treasure of true wisdom'. George Eliot recommended it in a letter dated 9 February 1849. In *The Mill on the Floss*, the *Imitatio* (Book Four, Chapter Three) comforts Maggie Tulliver; its message of selfless renunciation excites her and encourages her to adopt this way of life. It is thought that this echoed a period of religious devotion in Eliot's own youth. On a literary theme, Dame Agatha Christie's Miss Marple read a chapter of the *Imitatio* every night.

The *Imitatio* was certainly embraced in other circles. It was read enthusiastically by Dag Hammarskjöld, Secretary-General of the United Nations 1953–61, as well as by a former Prime Minister of Italy, Marco Minghetti (1818–86). It was in General Charles Gordon's possession during his various military campaigns. Charles-Geneviève d'Éon de Beaumont (1728–1810), diplomat, soldier and secret agent, requested to be buried with a crucifix and a copy of the *Imitatio*. One of Sir Edwin Landseer's paintings, *Man Proposes, God Disposes*, gained its title from a phrase in the *Imitatio*; the painting symbolized the loss of Sir John Franklin's entire polar expeditionary force in 1845. The *Imitatio*'s magnetism persists to the present day, with the writer Peter Ackroyd recently selecting it as his chosen book on a desert island.[68]

A TIMELESS CLASSIC

From the Late Middle Ages to the present day, the *Imitatio* has managed to capture the essence of the Christian spirit. Its appeal owes a great deal to its Biblicism. As Wesley remarked in the preface to his 1735 edition:

> And herein it greatly resembles the Holy Scriptures, that, under the plainest words, there is a divine, hidden virtue, continually flowing into the soul of a pious and attentive reader, and by the blessing of God, transforming it into his image.[69]

The *Imitatio*'s emphasis on submission to others and service to God sets a prominent theme: believers are expected to dwell on their own failings and weaknesses. They are called upon to examine their own spiritual state rather than seek fault in others: 'You readily excuse and explain your own activities, but you will not accept the explanations of others. It would be better to accuse yourself and to excuse your neighbours. If you want others to bear your burdens, you must put up with theirs.'[70] Readers are repeatedly drawn to the key theme of

humility, for which Christ's humanity provides the model. As
Christ remarks:

> Is it such a great thing for you, who are only dust and nothing, to
> submit yourself to another for God's sake, when I, the Almighty
> and the Most High, who created everything out of nothing, hum-
> bly submitted Myself to humanity for your sake? I became the
> humblest and least of all, so that through My humility you might
> overcome your pride. You, who are but dust, must learn to obey.[71]

The frailty of humanity is better understood in the light of
Christ's redemptive work: 'So ascribe nothing good to yourself
or anyone else, but attribute everything to God, without whom
you have nothing.'[72] As Ronald Knox remarked, this does not
make easy reading.[73] Believers are criticized for their hypocrisy,
professing Christianity in name but not in practice. This is
powerfully illustrated in a chapter entitled 'On the lack of
lovers of the Cross':

> Jesus has many who love His Kingdom of Heaven, but few who
> will carry His Cross. He has many who desire comfort, but few
> who desire suffering . . . Many want to rejoice with Him, but few
> will stay by Him. Many follow Jesus to the breaking of bread,
> but few will drink the cup of His suffering. Many admire His
> miracles, but few follow Him to the ignominy of the Cross. Many
> love Jesus as long as no hardship touches them.[74]

Devotional works like the *Imitatio* were adept at transcending theological divisions. All Christian denominations believe
that religious reform has little substance without spiritual
renewal; this sentiment is shared by the major world religions.
Given its contents and remarkable circulation and reception,
the *Imitatio Christi* remains one of the Christian world's most
powerful expressions of spirituality.

NOTES

1. Thomas à Kempis, tr. Knox, R., and Oakley, M., *The Imitation of Christ* (London: Sheed & Ward, 1959), pp. 7–8.

2. For the broader Late Medieval context, see R. N. Swanson, *Religion and Devotion in Europe, c.1215–c.1515* (Cambridge: Cambridge University Press, 1995).

3. The earliest extant manuscript produced in England was copied in 1438 by John Dygon, a member of the Sheen Charterhouse. For the broader context, see R. N. Swanson, *Catholic England* (Manchester: Manchester University Press, 1993); Eamon Duffy, *The Stripping of the Altars* (London and New Haven: Yale University Press, 1992).

4. The first edition included Lady Margaret Beaufort's translation of Book Four. In the Late Middle Ages, the *Imitatio* was adopted by an impressive list of political and ecclesiastical patrons: Philip the Good (1396–1467); Francisco Jiménez de Cisneros (1436–1517); Margaret of York (1446–1503); Louise of Savoy (1476–1531); Isabella of Portugal (1503–39); Katherine Parr (1512–48).

5. See Short Title Catalogue in Maximilian von Habsburg, *Catholic and Protestant Translations of the Imitatio Christi, 1425–1650* (Farnham: Ashgate, 2011), pp. 249ff.

6. Johnson wrote that it 'must be a good book, as the world has opened its arms to receive it'.

7. Peter Burke, 'Cultures of Translation in Early Modern Europe', in *Cultural Translation in Early Modern Europe*, ed. P. Burke and R. Po-chia Hsia (Cambridge: Cambridge University Press, 2007), p. 20. John Van Engen (tr.), *Devotio Moderna: Basic Writings* (New York: Paulist Press, 1988), p. 7.

8. See Eknath Easwaran, *Seeing with the Eyes of Love: On the Imitation of Christ* (Tomales: Nilgiri Press, 1996).

9. The 1427 manuscript is in the Royal Library in Brussels.

10. The three books (excluding Book Four) do not represent the three stages of the mystical process (purgative, illuminative and unitive), even though some later editors interpreted them in that manner.

11. J. van Ginneken argued that Grote provided the basic framework for the *Imitatio*, which was embellished by later copyists and, finally, polished by Kempis. See Pierre Debongnie and Jacques Huijben, *L'Auteur ou les auteurs de l'Imitation* (Louvain: Publications universitaires de Louvain, 1957), who argue persuasively in defence of Kempis' authorship.

12. Gerson and Kempis dominated the colophons and title pages between *c*.1471 and 1650. See von Habsburg, *Catholic and Protestant Translations*, pp. 249ff.

13. Nikolaus Staubach, 'Von der persönlichen Erfahrung zur Gemeinschaftsliteratur. Entstehungs- und Rezeptionsbedingungen geistlicher Reformtexte im Spätmittelalter', *Ons Geestelijk Erf* 68 (1994), p. 211. See also Stephanus Axters, *De Imitatione Christi* (Kempen-Niederrhein: Landkreis Kempen-Krefeld, 1971).

14. 'The *Imitatio* is not limited to one cultural epoch; like ecstatic contemplations of the All-One, it departs from all culture and belongs to no culture in particular. This explains its two thousand editions as well as the different suppositions concerning its author and its time of composition that fall into a range of three hundred years.' J. Huizinga, tr. Payton, R. J., and Mammitzsch, U., *The Autumn of the Middle Ages* (Chicago: University of Chicago Press, 1996), pp. 266–7.

15. The term *devotio moderna* was first coined in the 1420s by Henry Pomerius. See Regnerius Post, *The Modern Devotion* (Leiden: Brill, 1968), p. xi; Van Engen, *Devotio Moderna*, p. 7; John Van Engen, *Sisters and Brothers of the Common Life* (Philadelphia: University of Pennsylvania Press, 2008).

16. It is not helped by the fact that Post's magisterial study of the Modern Devotion includes the following statement: 'all four books were written for monastics and specifically monastics of the contemplative life'. Post, *Modern Devotion*, p. 533. The English novelist William Thackeray disliked the *Imitatio* on account of its monastic traits – 'written by a man in a cloister for other cloistered men'.

17. See in particular Kempis' *Sermons to the Novices Regular* (London: Kegan Paul, Trench, Truebner & Co., 1907).

18. For monastic references, see 1/xvii–xviii (Book One, Chapters Seventeen and Eighteen). For each reference to the *Imitatio*, I provide the book and chapter number.

19. See Axters, *De Imitatione Christi*.

20. It is littered with over 1,000 scriptural references, with the majority taken from the Psalms (*c*.140), the Book of Wisdom (*c*.60), the Prophets (*c*.40) and the Book of Job (24). Regarding the New Testament, there are more citations from St Paul than from the Four Evangelists (with 120 and 100 respectively). Other literary influences on the *Imitatio* include: Aristotle, Ovid, Seneca, St Gregory (329–89), St Augustine of Hippo (354–430), St Bernard of Clairvaux (1090–1153), Hugh of St Victor (1096–1141), St Bon-

aventure (1221–74), John van Ruysbroeck (1293–1381), Heinrich Eger von Kalkar (1308–1408) and Geert Grote.

21. See 1/i. For more references to the Bible, see also 1/v, 1/xx. All translations in this Introduction are quoted verbatim from this edition.

22. See 1/i.

23. See 1/ii.

24. For more references to learning, see 1/iii, 3/i–iv, 3/xxxi.

25. See 1/xix. For more examples of the *Imitatio*'s emphasis on interiority, see 1/i, 1/x–xi, 1/xvii–xviii, 2/i, 2/v–vi, 4/xi, 3/i, 3/xxxi, 3/xxxviii, 3/xlv.

26. See 1/xxii.

27. See 3/lii. There are explicit references to the Sacrament of Confession in 4/iii, vii, ix.

28. See 1/xxiii.

29. For more references to suffering and adversities, see 1/xii–xiii, 1/xviii, 1/xxi–xxii, 1/xxv, 2/i–ii, 2/vi, 2/ix–xii, 4/viii, 3/iii, 3/xviii–xx, 3/xxxv, 3/xlvii, 3/lvi.

30. Ludolph of Saxony's *Vita Christi* presented the concrete events of Christ's life, though it also included doctrinal and moral instructions.

31. See 2/i.

32. Van Engen, *Devotio Moderna*, p. 25.

33. See 4/xvii. For more references to Christ, see 1/i, 1/xxv, 2/i, 2/vii–viii, 2/xi–xii, 4/i, 4/viii, 3/iii, 3/v, 3/x, 3/xviii, 3/xxx, 3/xlii–xliii, 3/lvi, 3/lviii. For references to the Devil, see 1/xiii, 4/x, 3/vi, 3/xxxix.

34. See 3/lviii.

35. Johannes Busch described the Modern Devout as the new Desert Fathers. Mathilde Van Dijk, 'Disciples of the Deep Desert: Windesheim Biographers and the Imitation of the Desert Fathers', *Church History and Religious Culture* 86/4 (2006), p. 258. See also Kempis' biographies of the *devotio moderna*'s leading advocates, including Grote, Radewijns and Zutphen, and his *Chronicle of the Canons Regular*.

36. Jacopo da Voragine's (1230–98) *Golden Legend*, well known in Modern Devout circles, was the main reference work for saints' lives.

37. See 3/lviii.

38. For the *Imitatio*'s allusion to pilgrimages, see 4/i.

39. For more references to the saints, see 1/xi, 1/xviii–xix, 2/x, 3/xxxv, 3/xlvii, 3/lviii.

40. See 4/iii.

41. See 4/xi. See also 4/v.

42. See 4/ii. The phrase 'when you celebrate or hear the Mass' implies that priests celebrating the Mass and administering the Sacrament are not the only addressees.

43. The approximate timeframe for the Early Modern period is late 1400s/early 1500s to mid-1700s.

44. The *Imitatio* was also promoted by leading reformers such as St Teresa of Avila (1515–82), St Carlo Borromeo (1538–84) and St François de Sales (1567–1622). Georg Witzel (1501–73) is a particularly interesting figure, who translated the *Imitatio* into German. A lapsed Protestant, Witzel was a leading Catholic moderate in the 1530s and 1540s, seeking reconciliation between Protestants and Catholics.

45. By 1565, the Jesuits had twelve administrative provinces, ranging from Europe to Brazil, India and Ethiopia. By 1630, there were already 15,500 Jesuits.

46. The two most influential Latin editions by the Jesuits Henricus Sommalius (1534–1619) and Heribert Rosweyde (1569–1629) were first printed in Antwerp.

47. Creasy recalls how the *Imitatio* was dismissed as being 'hopelessly pre-Vatican II' by his clerical friends. William Creasy, *The Imitation of Christ* (Macon, Georgia: Mercer University Press, 1989), pp. xiii, xvi. The full title for *Gaudium et Spes* is *The Pastoral Constitution on the Church in the Modern World*. It addresses humanity's relationship to modern society and culture.

48. Joseph de Guibert, *The Jesuits* (St Louis: Institute of Jesuit Sources, 1986), pp. 156–7; John O'Malley, *The First Jesuits* (Cambridge, Massachusetts: Harvard University Press, 1993), p. 265.

49. Some scholars have anachronistically portrayed Kempis and/or the *Imitatio* as forerunners of the Protestant Reformation. Albert Hyma asserted that Kempis presented 'the fully fledged Calvinistic doctrine of predestination' in the *Imitatio*. Albert Hyma, *The Christian Renaissance* (Hamden, Connecticut: Archon Books, 1965), pp. 565, 603. More recently, an editor wrote: 'Although Thomas à Kempis died several years before Martin Luther was born, his belief that we are saved by God's grace through faith in Christ alone – and not through our works – set a stage for spiritual reformation and devised a standard of piety that would inspire Christians throughout all time.' Thomas à Kempis, *Imitation of Christ* (Nashville: Thomas Nelson Inc., 1999), pp. ix–x.

50. See 3/xxx.

51. See 3/liv and 3/lv.

52. See 3/l.

53. For more details on their appropriation of the *Imitatio* (with the exception of Arndt), see von Habsburg, *Catholic and Protestant Translations*. For Arndt, see Johann Arndt, *True Christianity*, and *Pietists: Selected Writings*, in the *Classics of Western Spirituality* series.

54. The Anabaptists were a radical group which emerged in the Swiss Confederation and Holy Roman Empire during the European Reformation. They challenged and rejected the Scriptural basis for infant baptism. The Family of Love (Familists) consisted of mystic, religious communities, which existed in the Low Countries and England.

55. David Crane, 'English translations of the *Imitatio Christi* in the Sixteenth and Seventeenth Centuries', *Recusant History* 13/2 (October 1975), pp. 79–84. Arminianism was the term given by their Puritan opponents to the High Churchmen of early-seventeenth-century England, of whom Lancelot Andrewes and William Laud were leading examples.

56. For the former see 1/xii, for the latter 2/iv. The religious sonnet 146 seems to come straight out of the *Imitatio*. I thank Peter Milward for all of these references. See also his *Catholicism of Shakespeare's Plays* (Southampton: Saint Austin Press, 1997), pp. 27, 106–7.

57. See *Bibliothèque de la Compagnie de Jésus*, ed. Carlos Sommervogel, 8 vols (Paris and Bruxelles: Oscar Schepens and Alphonse Picard, 1890–98) and Augustin de Backer, *Essai Bibliographique sur le livre De Imitatione Christi* (Liège: Heverlee, Editions de la Bibliothèque, 1864) for an overview of post-1650 Jesuit editions.

58. He was also the driving force behind the revision of the Douai-Rheims Bible.

59. Cited in Roland Hill, *Lord Acton* (London and New Haven: Yale University Press, 2000), p. 405.

60. Ibid.

61. Thomas Keble's brother, John (1792–1866) was one of the leading figures in the Oxford Movement. The English poet Matthew Arnold, John Keble's godson, described the *Imitatio* as 'the most exquisite document, after those of the New Testament, of all that the Christian spirit has ever inspired'.

62. See Chapters 6, 7 and 8 in von Habsburg, *Catholic and Protestant Translations*.

63. Frank Whaling (ed.), *John and Charles Wesley* (London: Paulist Press, 1981), p. 299.

64. Wesley's first edition in 1735 (and some later editions) was not abridged. The first abridged edition seems to be that of 1741, printed in London.

65. The omitted chapters are 1/vi, ix, xvii, xix, xxii. While Chapter Twenty-two alludes to the confession of sins, Chapter Six refers to the controlling of sensual and bodily desires. For my analysis of Wesley's version, I used John Wesley (ed.), *The Christian's Pattern* (London, 1741).

66. The omitted chapters include: 3/xii–xiii, xviii, xx, xxxii–xxxiii, xxxv–xxxvi, xxxix, xli, xliv–xlv, xlvii, li and liii.

67. Henry Rack, 'John Wesley', *ODNB*.

68. *Desert Island Discs*, BBC Radio 4, Sunday, 20 May 2012.

69. John Wesley (ed.), *The Christian's Pattern* (London, 1735).

70. See 2/iii.

71. See 3/xiii.

72. See 3/ix.

73. On that theme, Eknath Easwaran wrote: 'We need not let Thomas' medieval language alarm us here. He is saying only what Gandhi said: "I am the most ambitious man in the world: I want to make myself zero".' Easwaran, *Seeing with The Eyes of Love*, p. 243.

74. See 2/xi.

Note on the Translation

The Introduction explains the origins of the *Imitation of Christ* and demonstrates how many versions of the book throughout history have reflected the theological presuppositions of translators, who altered or removed various passages. This is also true of some modern translations. When Leo Sherley-Price made the 1952 translation for Penguin Classics, however, he faithfully translated the Latin text in full and this translation does the same, following the first printed version of *c*.1471.

An early alternative title for the *Imitation* was *Musica Ecclesiastica*, which reflected the fact that the simple Latin has a very rhythmic style. Dr Henry Parry Liddon, in his edition of 1890, tried to reflect this by putting the whole text into blank verse. (He also divided it up into sections so that a passage could be read every day of the year.) This translation is in prose, but it is hoped that the inherent rhythms and musicality of the original are still apparent, and that readers will be encouraged to read the text aloud, as would have often been the case in the past.

This new translation may be called 'ecumenical and gender-conscious' so that it can be read without anyone feeling excluded. The only exception to this is that God is still called 'He'. It also avoids the pseudo-Jacobean style that many earlier translators favoured; instead I have attempted to use language that is clear and direct. There are a large number of biblical references and quotations from many Classical and Christian writers in the text, and the notes identify the sources of these, as well as providing some clarifications to the text.

The book has been given different titles in various editions, but *The Imitation of Christ* has stuck. The concept of *imitation* needs some explanation, as the idea that we should imitate or copy Jesus might seem blasphemous to some. However, in the New Testament the word *imitate* is coterminous with the words '*follow*' and '*disciple*'. St Augustine posed the question: 'What is it to follow except to imitate?' Over the years the concept of imitation has changed. At one time it related to Christ's divinity but it later came to imply the imitation of Christ's humanity, following the ideas of St Bernard of Clairvaux (1090–1153) and the Franciscans.

Certain terms are key in à Kempis' text, and appear frequently in this translation. Several of these may need some brief explanation, with reference to à Kempis' worldview:

Grace: The activity of God in the lives of people. It is a freely given and undeserved gift that enables us to overcome our lower nature.

Comfort or consolation: Also a gift from God, which offers the soul a feeling of well-being and acceptance. This can be an emotional experience and one common for people starting off on the way of discipleship. À Kempis often refers to this feeling as a means of inspiring us but also as something that God can remove in order to make us more determined to stay on the path of spiritual discipline.

Conscience: The inner voice which encourages us to do good rather than evil.

Peace: A key biblical word, since peace is what Christ came to bring. The Hebrew word *shalom* indicates a wholeness and harmony of relations and has almost the same meaning as redemption. The soul that is at one with God is at peace.

The four books of the *Imitation* were originally issued separately and some versions never included Book Four, which concentrated on the Eucharist. This translation, as with some others, has reversed Books Four and Three in order to make a more coherent and satisfactory conclusion to the work. There is a logic here: Book Three may be called the 'Eschatological Book' because it leads the reader to consider death and emphasizes the ultimate triumph of God (Chapters 57–59). To avoid confusion, the sections are labelled as Parts, while the numbering of the Books remains the same.

The *Imitation* has not recently been read as frequently as it was in earlier times but it is our hope that this translation may lead new generations to discover in it a deep understanding of humanity and spirituality. I am grateful to those who gave me advice in this project, especially Ms Stacey Redman, The Very Revd John Drury, Professor Henry Mayr-Harting, Canon John Rogan, Fr Emmanuel Sullivan S.A., Fr Adam McCoy OHC and the Very Revd Jane Shaw. I would like to dedicate this volume to the Brothers of the Order of the Holy Cross at West Park, New York, where I first started this investigation into *The Imitation of Christ* in 1996, and whose support and love have sustained me on The Way.

Robert Jeffery
Oxford, July 2012

Further Reading

VERSIONS OF
THE IMITATION OF CHRIST

Creasey, W. (tr.) (Notre Dame, Ind.: Ave Maria Press, 1989)
Dudley, R. (tr.) (Wheathampstead: Anthony Clarke, 1980)
Gardiner, H. J., SJ (ed.) (New York: Image Books Doubleday, 1955)
 Knox, R., and Oakley, M. (tr.) (London: Sheed & Ward, 1959)
Wesley, J. (ed.), *The Christian's Pattern* (Halifax, NS: W. Milner, Kessinger Rare Reprint, 2008)

BOOKS REFERRED TO IN THE TEXT
AND FOR FURTHER STUDY

À Kempis, T., tr. Griffin, W., *Consolations for my Soul* (New York: Crossroads, 2005)
À Kempis, T., tr. Griffin, W., *Meeting the Master in the Garden* (New York: Crossroads, 2005)
Augustine, ed. Canning, R., *The Rule of St Augustine* (London: Darton, Longman & Todd, 1985)
Barton, S. (ed.), *Holiness Past & Present* (London: T&T Clarke, 2003)
Benedict, tr. and ed. White, C., *The Rule of St Benedict* (London: Penguin Classics, 2008)

Biggs, B. J. H., *The Imitation of Christ: The First English Translation* (Oxford: OUP, 1997)

Bonhoeffer, D., tr. Green, B. and Krans, R., ed. Kelly, G. B., and Godsey, J. D., *Collected Works, vol. 4: Discipleship* (Minneapolis: Fortress Press, 1996)

Burridge, R., *Imitating Jesus* (Michigan: Eerdmans, 2007)

Carroll, T. (ed.), *Jeremy Taylor: Selected Works* (New York: Paulist Press, 1990)

Chadwick, H. (tr.), *St Augustine's Confessions* (Oxford: OUP, 1992)

Constable, G., *Three Studies in Medieval Religious and Social Thought* (Cambridge: CUP, 1998)

Crane, D., 'English translations of the *Imitatio Christi* in the Sixteenth and Seventeenth Centuries', *Recusant History* 13/2 (October 1975)

Davies, J. G., *Pilgrimage Yesterday and Today* (London: SCM Press, 1988)

Duffy, E., *The Stripping of the Altars* (London and New Haven: Yale University Press, 1992)

Eliot, G., *The Mill on the Floss* (New York: The Modern Library, 2001)

French, R. M. (tr.), *The Way of a Pilgrim* (London: SPCK, 1986)

de Guibert, J., *The Jesuits* (St Louis: Institute of Jesuit Sources, 1986)

Hammarskjöld, D., *Markings* (London: Faber, 1963)

Hilton, W., ed. Sherley-Price, L. and Wolters, C., *The Ladder of Perfection* (London: Penguin, 1998)

Huizinga, J., *Erasmus and the Age of Reformation* (London: Phoenix Press, 2002)

Huizinga, J., tr. Hopman, F., *The Waning of the Middle Ages* (London: Penguin, 2002)

Ignatius Loyola, ed. Munitiz, J. and Endean, P., *Personal Writings* (London: Penguin Classics, 2004)

Jeffery, R., *Anima Christi* (London: Darton, Longman & Todd, 1994)

Kirk, K., *The Vision of God* (London: Longmans, 1956)

Kroll, J. and Bachrach, B., *The Mystic Mind* (New York: Routledge, 2005)

Lang, B., *Sacred Games: A History of Christian Worship* (London and New Haven: Yale University Press, 1997)

Lewis-Anthony, J., *Circles of Thorns* (London: Continuum, 2008)

Longenecker, R. N., *Patterns of Discipleship in the New Testament* (Michigan: Eerdmans, 1996)

Maas, R. and O'Donnell, G., *Spiritual Traditions for the Contemporary Church* (Nashville: Abingdon Press, 1995)

MacCulloch, D., *Reformation: Europe's House Divided 1490–1700* (London: Penguin, 2003)

McGuire, B. P. (tr.), *Jean Gerson: Early Works* (New York: Paulist Press, 1998)

Miles, M., *The Image and Practice of Holiness* (London: SCM Press, 1988)

Moltmann, J., tr. Wison, R. A. and Bowden, J. *The Crucified God* (London: SCM Press, 1974)

Morris, C., *The Discovery of the Individual 1050–1200* (London: SPCK, 1972)

O' Malley, J., *The First Jesuits* (Cambridge, Mass: Harvard University Press, 1993)

Post, R. R., *The Modern Devotion* (Leiden: Brill, 1968)

Segundo, J., *The Christ of the Ignatian Exercises* (London: Sheed & Ward, 1987)

Sumption, J., *Pilgrimage* (London: Faber, 2002)

Swanson, R. N., *Religion and Devotion in Europe, c. 1215–c.1515* (Cambridge: Cambridge University Press, 1995)

Tinsley, E. J., *The Imitation of God in Christ* (London: SCM Press, 1960)

Underhill, E., *Mysticism* (London: Methuen, 1911)

Van Engen, J., *Sisters and Brothers of the Common Life* (Philadelphia: University of Pennsylvania Press, 2008)

Van Engen, J. (tr.), *Devotio Moderna: Basic Writings* (New York: Paulist Press, 1988) von Habsburg, M., *Catholic and Protestant Translations of the Imitation of Christ 1425–1650* (Farnham: Ashgate, 2011)

de Voragine, J., tr. Ryan, W. G., with Introduction by Duffy, E., *The Golden Legend: Readings on the Saints* (Princeton: Princeton University Press, 2012)

Whaling, F. (ed.), *John and Charles Wesley: Selected Writings and Hymns* (New York: Paulist Press, 1981)

Woods, R. J., *Christian Spirituality* (New York: Orbis, 2006)

THE IMITATION
OF CHRIST

PART ONE

THE CHAPTERS OF
BOOK ONE

Here begins the advice helpful to
the spiritual life

ONE

Of the Imitation of Christ and despising the
futilities of the world

'Whoever follows me will not walk in darkness,' says our Lord.[1]

In these words, Christ calls us to imitate His life and conduct, if we desire true enlightenment and freedom from all hardness of heart.[2] So let our chief endeavour be to meditate on the life of Jesus Christ.

Jesus' teaching exceeds the teachings of all the Saints, so whoever has His Spirit will discover the secret heavenly manna.[3] But many people, although they often hear the Gospel, have little desire to follow it, because they do not have the Spirit of Christ in them.[4] Those who wish to understand and appreciate the words of Christ must strive to model the whole of their life on Him.

What use is it for learned people to discuss the doctrine of the Trinity if they have no humility, and so displease the Trinity?[5] Learned words do not make anyone wise or holy; it is a good life which draws us closer to God. I would rather feel deep sorrow than be able to define it. If you knew the whole Bible by heart and the teachings of all the philosophers, what good would that be without the grace and love of God? 'Vanity of Vanities – all is vanity'[6] except to love and serve God alone.[7] And it is supreme wisdom to come daily nearer to the Kingdom of Heaven by despising the world.

It is futile to seek for riches or public approval.

It is futile to be a slave to bodily desires[8] and to crave for things which will have bad consequences.

It is futile to desire a long life if you do not wish for a good life.

It is futile to think only about this world and to ignore eternal life.

It is futile to love temporary things and not to move towards the place of everlasting joy.

Keep constantly in mind the saying, 'The eye is not satisfied with seeing or the ear filled with hearing.'[9] Strive to remove your heart from the love of visible things, and direct your concerns to invisible things. For those who follow their natural inclinations defile their conscience, and fall away from the grace of God.

TWO

On personal humility

Naturally everyone desires knowledge,[1] but what use is that without a sense of the mystery of God? A humble peasant who serves God is more pleasing to God than a conceited intellectual who knows the course of the stars but ignores the things of the spirit.[2] Those with real self-knowledge realize their own worthlessness, and do not enjoy public approbation. If I possess all the knowledge in the world, but have no love,[3] it will not assist me when God judges my actions. Avoid excessive desire for knowledge, which will lead to much perplexity and deception. Intellectuals wish to appear to be learned and to be widely respected for their wisdom. But knowledge of a great many things has no spiritual advantage. Many words do not satisfy the soul, but a good life refreshes the mind; and a clear conscience[4] leads to confidence in God.

The more complete and the better your knowledge, the stricter will be the judgement on you, unless you lead a holy life. So do not be proud of any skill or knowledge you may possess, but respect the learning that you have. If it appears that you know a great deal and have deep interest in many things, remember that there are many other matters where you are very ignorant. So put away your pride and admit your ignorance.[5] Why do you wish to consider yourself above others, while there are many people who are wiser and more perfect in the law of God? If you want to know or learn anything for your personal gain, then rejoice in being unknown and unregarded.

A realistic and humble attitude is the highest and most valuable thing we can learn. The wisest form of self-understanding is to think little of ourselves and to think kindly and well of others. If you see someone doing evil, or carrying out a wrong act, do not for that reason think you are better than they; for you cannot tell how long you will remain in a state of grace. We are all frail; remember that no one is frailer than you.

THREE

On teaching the truth

The happy person is not edified by omens and passing appearances[1] but by truth itself, as it is in reality. Our own conjectures and observations often mislead us, and we learn very little. Of what value is specious reasoning on deep and obscure matters, when we are not going to be judged by our knowledge of such things? It is supreme folly to neglect things that are useful and vital, and deliberately turn to those that are curious and harmful. Actually 'we have eyes but do not see'.[2] What do origins and appearances really matter to us?

Ultimately it is the Eternal Word which speaks to us. It is from that Word that all things come into being,[3] and all things speak of Him. It is the author of all things who speaks to us.[4] Without Him no one can judge anything rightly. It is those who see all things as one, and who relate everything to the One God, and who see everything as in Him, who are able to remain single-minded and live at peace with God.

O God, the Living Truth,[5] unite me to Yourself in everlasting love![6] Frequently, I am wearied by all that I hear and read. All that I really desire and long for lies in You alone. So may all teachers keep silence, and let all creation stand still in Your presence. May You, and You alone, speak to us Your Word.[7]

The more closely we are united to You in simplicity, the more varied and profound will be the matters we grasp without effort. For we receive illumination and understanding from heaven. However hectic life becomes, the single-minded, simple and humble person will not become distracted; for everything will be done to God's glory. It is the undisciplined passions of your own heart which harm and hinder what you are doing. A good and devout person puts priorities in order, so that whatever task is being done, none will be an occasion for sin, but everything will be subjected to the dictates of sound judgement. The person who is trying to achieve self-mastery has the fiercest struggle.[8] But it must be our main priority to conquer the self, and to advance in holiness by growing stronger every day.[9]

All achievements in this life contain a level of imperfection. All our speculations include an element of darkness. A humble self-understanding is a safer way to God than a profound knowledge of academic disciplines. Learning in itself is not to be blamed, nor can we despise the acquisition of knowledge (for true learning is good in itself and comes from God), but a good conscience and a holy life are even better. Because people prefer to acquire knowledge rather than to live well, they often go astray and so bear little fruit.[10] If only such people were as concerned to uproot vices and replace them with virtues, as they are to share in learned discourses, there would not be so much dissolution and scandal among us, nor slackness in Religious Communities.[11] On the Day of Judgement we shall not be asked what we have read, but what we have done; not how eloquently we have spoken, but how holy our lives have been. Where now are the once well-known teachers and philosophers who were famous for their learning? They are hardly ever remembered, and others now occupy their seats. In their lifetime they seemed to be very important, but now no one speaks of them.[12]

How swiftly the glories of this world pass away![13] If only people's conduct had been as admirable as their learning, their study and reading would have been of real value! Many in this world care little for the service of God and their lives end up in futility. They perish through their own ambition, because they chose to be famous rather than humble.[14] The truly great are humble in mind, and consider public acclamations to be worthless. In order to find Christ, the truly wise consider all earthly things to be rubbish.[15] The really wise surrender their own wills to the will of God.

FOUR

On caution in our actions

We should not believe every word or impulse[1] but we should carefully and patiently examine whether they are in accordance with the will of God. Human nature is so weak that evil rather than good is more often believed[2] and spoken about others. But the wise do not willingly believe every tale that is told, for they know that people love gossip and that words can be careless.[3]

It is much better to avoid being precipitate in our actions, or clinging strongly to our own opinions. We should not believe all that we hear, nor gossip about what we hear of others. Listen to wise and sensible advice[4] and be guided by someone who is better than you, rather than following your own opinions. Experienced people understand what they are talking about.[5] The more humble and pleasing we are to God, the more we are at peace in all that we are doing.

FIVE

On reading the Holy Scriptures

When you read Holy Scripture, look for truth rather than fine words. It should be read in the spirit in which it was written. We should seek food for our souls rather than subtleties of speech, and we would do well to read simple devotional books rather than those which are very intellectual. Do not be influenced by the importance of the author, whether that person has a great reputation or not, but by the desire for the truth which attracts you. Do not ask, 'Who said that?'[1] but pay attention to what is said.[2]

People pass away, but the faithfulness of the Lord lasts for ever.[3] God speaks to us in many and varied ways[4] and He is no respecter of persons.[5] When reading the Scriptures, our curiosity often hinders us, for we try to examine and dispute matters which it would be better either to ignore or simply accept. If you wish to benefit, read with humility, simplicity and faith and have no desire to appear learned. Always ask questions and listen in silence to the words of the Saints. Listen to the parables of the Fathers,[6] for they are told for good reasons.

SIX

On controlling desires

If we have excessive desires, we become restless. The proud and the greedy are never at rest; but the poor and the humble rejoice in great peace. If you are not really dead to yourself, you will be tempted easily and succumb to insignificant and worthless things. The weak in spirit will be inclined to sensual and bodily desires. This makes them miserable and introverted and they become angry when they are despised. But those who obtain what they desire will soon be stricken with remorse, because they have given in to their desires. This does not assist us in a search for peace. True peace of heart can only be found in resisting the passions, not by giving in to them. The worldly, who do things for show, will find no peace. Peace is for those who are strongly devout.

SEVEN

On avoiding false confidence and conceit

Those who put their trust in animals or people are very fool-ish.[1] For Christ's sake, do not fear to be the servant of others, nor to seem to be poor in the world. Do not trust yourself but put your whole trust in God.[2] Do all you can, and God will bless your good intentions. Do not trust in your intellectual ability nor in the cleverness of anyone else, but trust in the grace of God, who helps the humble[3] and humbles the proud.

If you have possessions or influential friends, do not boast of them, but only give glory to God.[4] He gives us all things and desires above all that we should give ourselves to Him. Do not be proud of your physical strength or beauty, which sickness could spoil or disfigure. Do not be proud of your own ability or cleverness, which will offend God, who has showered on us all our natural gifts. Do not think that you are better than others, or you will appear worse in the eyes of God, who alone knows the secrets of our hearts.[5]

Do not boast of your good deeds, for God does not judge as the world does; and what delights us often displeases God.[6] You need to remain humble and remember that if you have any good qualities, others may have more. It is good for you to esteem others as better than yourself, but it does you great harm if you put yourself above others. True peace lies in humil-ity; those who are proud are always full of pride and jealousy.

EIGHT

Of the dangers of intimacy[1]

Do not tell others what is on your mind[2] but seek advice from someone who is wise and fears God. Keep company with young people or strangers sparingly. Do not admire the wealthy, and avoid the company of celebrities. It is better to keep company with the poor and simple, the devout and the virtuous, and talk to them about uplifting matters. Avoid undue familiarity with the opposite sex, but commend all good women to God. Seek to be familiar only with God and His Angels, rather than human company.

We must live in charity with everyone, but intimacy with them is not desirable. Sometimes we meet a public celebrity, but we will not be impressed. Equally, we may think that we are good company when, in fact, our bad behaviour offends other people.

NINE

On obedience and discipline

It is a good thing to live under obedience to a Superior and not to be one's own master. It is much safer to obey than to rule. Many live under obedience more out of necessity than love, and such people often complain and are discontented. They will never find freedom of mind, unless they are totally submissive in their hearts and in their love of God. Wherever you go you will not find rest, except in humble obedience to the rule of a Superior.[1] Having fantasies about other places and wanting a change unsettles people.

We gladly do the things we enjoy, and keep company with the like-minded; but, if Christ is to live among us, we must sometimes surrender our own opinions for the sake of peace. No one is wise enough to know everything. So do not have confidence in your own views, but listen to the ideas of others. If your opinion is right but you surrender it for the love of God and follow another, you will win great merit. I have often heard that it is better to accept advice than to give it. It may be that two opinions are equally good but it is a sign of pride and obstinacy to refuse to come to an agreement with others when it is required.

TEN

On avoiding gossip

Stay away from public meetings as much as you can, for even with the best of intentions discussion of mundane matters can be a distraction, as we are easily corrupted and ensnared by vanity. I often wish that I had remained silent and had not been with others. Why is it that we injure our consciences when we are ready to chatter and gossip with each other, but seldom resort to silence? The reason we are so fond of talking with others is that we find it consoling and it refreshes a weary heart. We enjoy thinking and speaking of those things we like or desire, and equally of those we dislike. It is of no avail, for such outward consolation is a severe obstacle to inner and divine consolation.

We must watch and pray[1] so that we do not make bad use of our time. When it is right to speak, do so to offer enlightenment.[2] Bad habits and neglect of devotional progress are the chief reasons for failing to guard our tongues.[3] But committed conversation on spiritual matters helps our spiritual progress greatly, especially with those who share a common mind in the service of God.[4]

ELEVEN

On peace and spiritual progress

We could enjoy much peace if we were not bothered by what other people say and do, for they are no concern of ours. We cannot remain at peace if we meddle in other people's affairs or if we find the opportunity to rush about and make little or no attempt at recollection. Blessed are the pure in heart[1] for they will enjoy much peace.

How did some of the Saints become so perfect and contemplative? It is because they strove with all their might to suppress in themselves all earthly desires and so to cling to God in their inmost heart and offer themselves willingly and fully to Him. But we are gripped too much by our passions and are over-concerned with the passing affairs of the world. It is seldom that we fully master any small fault and we do not have enough zeal for our daily progress. So we remain spiritually cold or tepid.

If we were completely dead to self and free from inner conflict, we could taste divine things, and gain the experience of heavenly contemplation. But the greatest, and indeed the biggest, obstacle to our advance is that we are not free from our passions and lusts. Nor do we make any effort to follow the perfect way of the Saints. When we encounter a small trouble, we are quickly discouraged and turn to human consolation.

If, like brave heroes, we endeavoured to stand firm in battle we should not fail to experience the help of our Lord from heaven. He is always ready to help those who fight, trusting in His grace. He also gives us opportunities to fight victoriously. If we rely only on outward religious observances, our devotion will rapidly fade away. But let us put the axe to the root[2] so that, cleansed from our passions, we may possess our souls in peace.

If we could just root out one fault each year we would soon gain perfection. But, alas, the opposite is often the case. Frequently we are often better and purer at the beginning of our conversion than after many years in religious vows. Our fervour and virtue should grow daily; but it is now considered a good thing if someone retains even a small part of their early zeal. If only we would begin by strongly disciplining ourselves[3] then we would be able later to do everything easily and gladly.

It is hard to give up old habits and harder still to conquer our own wills. But if you cannot triumph in small and easy things, how can you succeed in big things?[4]

From the start, resist your evil inclinations and break off evil habits for fear that you are led into greater difficulties. If only you could know what great peace for yourself and what great joy for your friends your efforts would win, you would take even more care of your spiritual progress.

TWELVE

On the uses of adversity

From time to time, it is good for us to encounter troubles and adversities, for troubles compel us to search our hearts. It reminds us that we are strangers here[1] and that we can have no hope of anything in this world. Also, we benefit when we face opposition, and when people think badly of us and misjudge us, even when we do and mean well. Such things assist our humility and preserve us from pride and empty glory. When others despise us and think no good of us, we more readily turn to the inner judgement of God.

Therefore we should place such complete trust in God that we need no human comfort. When good people are troubled, tempted or disturbed by evil thoughts, they come to realize more clearly than ever that they need God, without whom we can do nothing.[2] Then, amid our misfortunes, we grieve and lament greatly and turn to prayer. Those who are weary of life long for the liberation of death, so that they may depart and be with Christ.[3] It is then that we know fully that in this life there can be no total security, nor perfect peace.

THIRTEEN

On resisting temptations

As long as we live in this world, we will always face trial and temptation.[1] As Job says, 'Do not human beings have a hard service on earth.'[2] Therefore we must be on guard against temptations and be watchful in prayer[3] so that the Devil has no means of deceiving us; for he never rests, but prowls around seeking someone to devour.[4] No one is so perfect and holy that they cannot be tempted, and we can never be safe from temptations.

Although temptations are so troublesome and grievous, they are also profitable for us. Through them we are humbled, cleansed and edified. All the Saints went through many hardships[5] and benefited from them; but those who could not resist temptations became reprobate and fell away.[6] There is no Religious Community so holy, no place so secluded that it is without adversities and temptations.

As long as we live, we will never be without temptations. The root of temptation lies within our own nature, because we are born with a tendency to evil.[7] When one temptation comes to an end, another takes its place. We shall always have something to resist, for we have lost the blessing of innocent happiness. Those who fly from temptations will encounter them more fiercely, for no one can gain a victory simply by running away. It is only through patience and true humility that we can grow stronger than our enemies.

If we just avoid superficial evil but fail to tear out its roots in ourselves, we will gain very little. In fact, temptations will return quickly and we will find ourselves in a worse state than before.[8] Slowly and by fortitude and patience[9] we can triumph by God's help rather than by our own violence and assertiveness. When you are tempted seek regular advice, and do not treat harshly those who suffer temptation. Rather, offer them the sort of encouragement that you would value yourself.

All evil temptation begins with an unstable mind and a lack of trust in God. Just as a ship without a helm is tossed about by the waves,[10] so are those who are careless and lose direction tempted in many ways. As the furnace tests iron, when it is being tempered,[11] so temptation tests the just. Often we do not know what we can tolerate, but temptation reveals our true nature. At the start of temptation we have to be especially on our guard, for the Enemy can be more easily overcome if he is unable to open the door to our minds. He must be refused entry as soon as he knocks. Hence the saying: 'Resist from the beginning; the medicine may not arrive in time.'[12]

Firstly, an evil thought crosses the mind; then comes a strong imagination; then delight and the desire to do evil and in the end we consent. So, if he is not resisted from the beginning, the Enemy gains complete mastery. The longer a lazy person delays, the weaker is resistance and the stronger is the power of the Enemy.

Some people face their deepest temptations soon after their conversion; for some it comes at the end of life; others are troubled throughout their lives; while there are those whose temptations are light. This is in accordance with the wisdom and justice of God's ways, who measures the condition and virtues of us all and provides all things for the salvation of those whom He chooses.

So when we are tempted we must not despair, but earnestly pray to God in the hour of need. For as St Paul says, 'When the test comes, God will at the same time provide a way out so that you may be able to endure it.'[13] So let us humble ourselves under the hand of God[14] in every trial and tribulation, for He will save and raise on high the lowly.[15] In all these trials our progress is being tested, so we may secure great merit and our virtue will be revealed. If, when we are without trials, we reveal great devotion, that is not so significant; but we can make great spiritual progress if we show patience in adversity. Some people are spared major temptations but are overtaken by small ones every day, so that they may be humble and learn to avoid trusting in themselves and recognize their frailty.

FOURTEEN

On avoiding rash judgements

Judge yourself, but avoid passing judgement on others.[1] In judging others, we spend our energy to no good purpose. We are often mistaken and so we sin; but it is a beneficial exercise to examine ourselves. Frequently, our personal feelings influence our judgement, and if we are encouraged by personal motives it may become a false judgement. If God were the only and constant object of our desires, we would not be so upset when our own opinions are rejected.

Frequently, we are drawn to act on the basis of an inner impulse or outward attraction. Many people are influenced in their actions through self-interest, but they may not be conscious of it. As long as events fit in with their own desires, they seem to enjoy full peace of mind, but when things fall out differently they become distressed and disconsolate. Similarly differences of opinion or belief can often be the cause of quarrels among friends and neighbours and even among Religious and devout people.

It is hard to break old habits and no one is easily weaned from their own opinions. If you rely on your own reasoning and ability rather than submit your will to Jesus Christ,[2] you will rarely and slowly attain wisdom. For it is God's will that we become fully obedient to Him and that we overcome mere reason on the wings of a burning love for Him.

FIFTEEN

On deeds inspired by love

Nothing in the world, nor affection for anyone, can justify doing evil. But in helping someone in need, we may put aside a good deed, so that a better one may be done in its place. For by doing this, the good deed is not lost, but changed for one that is better. Our outward deeds are of no value without love; but whatever is done out of love, however small, is totally fruitful. For God takes account of the greatness of our motives rather than the greatness of our achievements.

Whoever loves much, does much. Whoever does something well, does much. It is good to serve the community before serving our own interests. Often an apparently loving action can spring from selfish motives; for natural inclination, self-will, hope of reward and our own self-interest will rarely be entirely absent.

Whoever is inspired by true and perfect love is never self-seeking, but wishes only to serve the glory of God in all things. Those who seek no selfish pleasure will envy no one. Those who desire above all to merit God's blessing will not act out of self-gratification. We should ascribe no good to humanity but only to God, from whom all things come, who is their origin[1] and in whom all the Saints enjoy perfection and peace. If only we had a spark of true love in our hearts, we would know for certain that all earthly things are futile.

SIXTEEN

On living with the faults of others

If we are unable to correct ourselves, or others, we should wait patiently until God decides otherwise. It is perhaps good to think that this is better, so that our patience is tested, without which our merits are of little value. Whenever such obstacles hinder you, pray to God that He may grant you His help, and give you grace to endure them with a good heart.[1]

If someone who has been warned once or twice remains stubborn, do not dispute with them but commend all things to God that His will may be done, and His name hallowed[2] in all His servants. God knows perfectly well how to bring good out of evil.[3] Strive to be patient, bear with the faults and frailties of others, for you also have many faults which others have to tolerate. If you cannot mould yourself as you would wish, how can you expect other people to be entirely to your liking? For we expect other people to be perfect, but we do not correct our own faults.

We like to see others severely reprimanded, but we are unwilling to be corrected ourselves. We wish to restrict the liberty of others, but are not willing to be denied anything ourselves. We like to see others controlled by rules, yet we will not restrict ourselves. So it is very clear that we rarely consider our neighbour in the same light as ourselves. Yet if we were all perfect, what would we have to tolerate in others for Christ's sake?

For God has designed things so that we may learn to bear one another's burdens.[4] There is no one without faults and none without burdens.[5] We are not sufficient in ourselves.[6]

We are not wise in ourselves.[7] So we must support one another,[8] be tolerant of each other,[9] help, teach and advise one another. It is in times of trouble that we really discover the true value of our helpers. They do not weaken us, but reveal their true nature.

SEVENTEEN

On the monastic life

If you wish to live in peace and harmony with others, you must learn to discipline yourself in many ways. It is not easy to live in a Religious Community and remain there without fault[1] and faithfully persevere unto death.[2] Those who live this life happily to the end are greatly blessed. If you wish to achieve stability[3] and grow in grace, remember that you are a stranger and pilgrim on this earth.[4] If you wish to be a Religious, it is enough to be accounted a fool for Christ's sake.[5]

Having a tonsure and a habit are in themselves of little significance.[6] It is the transformation of your way of life and the total mortification of the senses that makes a true Religious. Those who seek anything in life, other than God and personal salvation, will find nothing but trouble and sadness.[7] Nor will we remain at peace if we cease to be the least and the servant of all.[8]

You have come here to obey orders, not to give orders. Remember you are called to work and service, not to pass your time in idleness and gossip, for in this life we are tried like gold in the furnace.[9] No one can remain here, unless they are ready to humble themselves with their whole being for the love of God.

EIGHTEEN

On the example set us by the Holy Fathers

Think about the glowing examples of the Holy Fathers, from whom shone true religion and perfection. Compared with them, we do little or nothing. Compared with them, our life is sadly lacking. The Saints and friends of Christ served our Lord in hunger and thirst, in cold and nakedness, in toil and weariness; in watching and fasting, in prayer and contemplation, in persecutions and many insults.[1]

The tribulations endured by the Apostles, Martyrs, Confessors, Virgins and others who strove to follow the footsteps of Christ were countless and endless. They all hated their lives in this world, so that they might gain eternal life.[2] How strict and self-denying were the lives of the Holy Fathers in the desert! How long and grievous the temptations they endured. How often they were assaulted by the Devil! How frequent and fervent their prayers to God! How strict their fasts! How great their zeal and ardour for spiritual progress! How valiant the battles they fought to overcome their vices! How pure and upright their intention towards God!

All day long they laboured and all night long they prayed continuously. Even as they worked, they never stopped praying.[3]

They used their time well; every hour seemed short in God's service. Through sweet contemplation, often they even forgot their bodily needs.

They renounced all riches, dignities, honours, friends and relations; they wanted to possess nothing in this world.

They would accept the necessities of life and bodily needs only with reluctance. Thus, though lacking in worldly goods, they were very rich in grace and virtue. Outwardly they were poor, but inwardly they were enriched by grace and heavenly consolation.

They were strangers to the world, but to God they were dear and familiar friends.[4] In their own eyes they were nothing, but in the eyes of God they were precious and beloved. Established in true humility, they lived in simple obedience. They walked in love and patience[5] and so daily increased in the Spirit and received great grace from God. They were given as an example to all Religious and they should encourage us to move forward in holiness, unlike the lukewarm people who encourage us in laxity.

When the communities were established how deep was the fervour of the Religious! How great was their devotion in prayer and their zeal for virtue! How strict was their observance of the Rule. What reverence and obedience was shown to the orders of the Superiors in those days! Their examples still reveal that there were indeed holy and perfect people, who fought valiantly and trampled the world under their feet. Nowadays, anyone who does not break rules or is very obedient is regarded as outstanding!

Oh, the negligence and coldness of the present time! Sloth and lukewarmness make life wearisome for us, and we soon lose our initial enthusiasm! May the desire to grow in grace not remain asleep in you, who have been honoured to contemplate so many examples of the devout life.

NINETEEN

*On practices suitable for those
in the Religious Life*

The life of a good Religious should shine with all the virtues, so that what appears outwardly to others is matched by inward practices. Indeed, there should be far more inward goodness than that which appears outwardly; for God searches all hearts.[1] We must respect Him above all things and live purely in His sight, like the Angels. Each new day we should renew our commitment and exert ourselves to devotion, as if it were the first day of our conversion, and say 'Help me, O Lord God, in my good resolution and in Your holy service; help me to start this day perfectly, for so far I have achieved nothing.'

Our intentions will reveal our spiritual progress and, if we wish to go far, we will need strong perseverance. Even someone with firm determination often encounters failure; and someone who rarely makes any firm commitment will not achieve anything. We fail in our intentions in many ways, and the casual omission of our spiritual exercises rarely passes without detriment to our souls. Even the commitment of holy people depends more on the grace of God than on their own wisdom, and they put their whole trust in Him in all they do. 'The human mind plans the way but the Lord directs the steps.'[2] And 'the way of human beings is not in their control, mortals, as they walk, cannot direct their steps'.[3]

If, in order to perform some act of kindness or to help someone, any of our spiritual exercises are omitted they can be resumed later. But if they are set aside casually, out of laziness or carelessness, this is inexcusable and will be harmful to our souls. However hard we try, we shall still fail too easily in many things. Even so we should always have a strong resolve, especially against those faults that most hinder our progress. There should be a careful scrutiny and organization of both our inward and outward life, since both are essential to our growth.

Although we cannot always preserve our recollection, yet we should do so from time to time, and at least once every day, either in the morning or the evening. Shape your intentions in the morning and at night review your behaviour (what you have done, said and thought during the day), for in all of these things you may have offended both God and your neighbour. Arm yourself strongly against the wickedness of the Devil.[4] If you control your appetite you will more easily control your bodily desires. Never be entirely idle but be occupied through reading, or writing, prayer and meditation, or in some work for the common good. But be discreet in practising physical mortification[5] for this is not for everybody. Non-essential spiritual exercises should not be done in public; for whatever is purely personal is best done in private.

Do not become casual about the community observances, by putting your personal devotions as a priority. But when you have fully and faithfully fulfilled your obligations, if there is time left over, use it for your own prayer. Not everyone prays in the same way. One pattern suits one person and a different devotion another. Also, the seasons require different devotions; some are best for festivals and others for ordinary days. When we are tempted, a suitable devotion may help; at other times we need peace and quietness. Some are suitable when we are sad and others when we are full of joy in the Lord.

We should renew our spiritual exercises on major festivals and ask the Saints for their prayers more fervently than ever. Between festivals we should resolve to live as if we were about to leave this world and come to the Heavenly Feast. So we should carefully prepare ourselves during the holy seasons and live even more devoutly, keeping every observance more strictly, as if we were about to receive the reward for our labours from God Himself. But if the reward is delayed, we should realize that we are not yet worthy of the greater glory, which will be revealed to us at the appointed time.[6] So let us prepare ourselves better for our departure from this world. 'Blessed is that slave whom his master will find at work when he arrives,' says St Luke the Evangelist; 'Truly I tell you, he will put that one in charge of all his possessions.'[7]

TWENTY

On the love of solitude and silence

Set aside a suitable time for recollection and regularly consider the loving kindness of God. Do not read out of curiosity or just to pass the time, but read those things which stir your heart to adoration. If you keep away from casual talk and aimless visits, listening to novelties and gossip, you will find plenty of time to spend in meditation on holy things. Whenever they could, the Saints avoided society and preferred to serve God in solitude.

A wise man wrote, 'As often as I have been among men, I have returned home a lesser man.'[1] We share this experience when we spend a lot of time in conversation. It is easier to be completely silent than not to talk more than we should. It is easier to be silent at home than to be careful about what we say in public. So whoever is determined to live an inward and spiritual life must withdraw from the crowd to be with Jesus.[2] No one can live in the public eye without harm to the soul, unless they want total obscurity. Only those who are happy to be silent can safely speak in public. Only those who have learned to obey can safely give orders. Only those who demonstrate a good conscience are able to celebrate.

The composure of the Saints was grounded in the fear of God, nor were they less careful and humble because they had outstanding virtues and kindness. But the negligence of the wicked emerges from pride and presumption and it leads to self-deception. Never promise yourself confidence in this life, even though you seem to be a good Religious or a holy hermit.

Those who are seen as public celebrities are the most exposed to serious peril, because they have far too much self-confidence.

Hence it is better not to be without temptation, and to be tested in order to avoid becoming composed and full of pride or to turn too easily to the comforts of the world. We would have a good conscience if we never ran off after passing pleasures, or were preoccupied with worldly affairs. If only we could reject fruitless anxiety, and just think about the things of God and salvation, how much peace and tranquillity we would have.

None of us are worthy of heavenly consolation unless we have spent time in devout penitence. If you want deep penitence, enter your room[3] and shut out the noise of the world; as it is written, 'Let awe restrain you, while you rest, meditate in silence.'[4] Inside your room you will discover what you will lose frequently outside. The continuous occupation of the room becomes a delight, but if it is ill-kept it will lead to weariness of spirit. If, from the beginning of your Religious Life, you have lived in your room and kept it well, it will later become a friend and a welcome comfort.

The devout soul benefits from quietness and silence and so learns the hidden secrets of the Scriptures.[5] There, in floods of tears, the soul can be washed and cleansed.[6] The more the soul withdraws from the noise of the world, the nearer the soul draws to her Creator. For God and His Holy Angels will come close to those who go apart from friends and acquaintances. It is better to live in obscurity and to seek one's salvation than to neglect it, even to work miracles. It is best for the Religious not to go out and about, and to avoid seeing others, rather than being seen by them.

Why do you want to admire and seek things you do not possess? The world with all its allurements is passing away.[7] Sensual desires want us to rush about, but when it is over what do you bring back except a spoiled conscience and a distracted heart? A cheerful departure often leads to a sad homecoming, and a merry evening will lead to a miserable morning. Every bodily pleasure may flow smoothly, but in the end it will bite like a snake and poison like a cobra.[8]

What can you see elsewhere that you cannot see here?[9] Look at the sky, the earth and all the natural elements – God made them all. What you see anywhere under the sun will only last for a little time. Possibly you hope for full satisfaction, but that cannot be achieved. If you could see the whole of existence in front of you, it would be nothing but an empty shadow.[10] Look to heaven, look to God[11] and seek forgiveness for your neglect and your sins. Leave empty matters to the empty-headed and pay attention to the things God commands you to do. Close the door and call upon the beloved Jesus.[12] Stay with Him in your room, for you will not find peace anywhere else. If you had never gone out and gossiped you would be much more at peace, and not suffering from a disturbed mind.

TWENTY-ONE

On true penitence

If you wish to grow in holiness, you must live in the fear of the Lord.[1] Do not look for lots of freedom, but train your senses and do not take up trivial activities. Rather, if you want to find true holiness, devote yourself to penitence. Dissipation will blind us to the many good things which penitence will reveal to us. If we consider our state of exile and the many perils which test our souls, it is amazing that anyone can feel completely contented with this life.

Frivolity and neglecting our faults will make us insensible to the real sorrows of our soul. So when we should be weeping, we engage in empty laughter. The only way to find true freedom and joy is in the fear of God and a clear conscience. Those who are happy can set aside every restricting distraction and concentrate on the main purpose of penitence. Those who reject whatever smears or weighs down their conscience are happy. Fight bravely, for one habit overcomes another. If you are willing to leave other people alone, they will gladly leave you alone to achieve your purposes.

Do not bother yourselves with other people's affairs, nor concern yourself with the affairs of your Superiors. Watch yourself at all times, and discipline yourself before you lecture your friends. If you do not enjoy popularity, do not feel sorry for yourself; rather be sorry that you are not living as well and as carefully as is appropriate to a servant of God and a devout Religious. Frequently, it is better and safer not to enjoy many bodily comforts in this life. But if we rarely or never feel God's consolation, it is our own fault because we have not sought to be penitent, nor given up all vain and worldly comforts.

Think of yourself as unworthy of divine consolation but actually deserving of considerable suffering. If we are really contrite, the present world becomes painful and bitter to us. A good person always finds reason for sorrow and tears, for if we think about our neighbours or ourselves, we know that in this life no one can live without trouble. The more strictly we examine ourselves, the more reason there is for sorrow. Our sins and vices are grounds for rightful sorrow and contrition of heart; for they have such a strong hold over us that we are rarely able to contemplate heavenly things.

If you had more concern for a holy death than for a long life, you would certainly desire to live better. If you were to consider carefully the pains of hell and purgatory[2] you would willingly endure toil and sorrow and would not shrink from hardships. But because such reflections do not move our hearts, we remain cold and unresponsive and cling to our old vanities.

Often it is our lack of spiritual life that enables our wretched body to rebel so easily. So humbly pray to our Lord to give you the spirit of penitence and say with the Prophet, 'You have fed them with the bread of tears, and given them tears to drink in full measure.'[3]

TWENTY-TWO

On human misery

Wherever you are and wherever you go you will find no happiness until you turn to God. Why are you so disturbed when things do not go the way you want them to? Does anyone enjoy everything they wish for? Neither do you, nor I, nor anyone else on this earth. In this life no one goes without trouble and anxiety, not even a Monarch or a Pope. Who then is the happiest person? Surely someone who is able to suffer for the love of God.

Many weak and foolish people[1] say, 'See what a good life that man enjoys! He is so rich, so great, so powerful, so distinguished!' But look up to the riches of heaven, and realize that all the riches of this world are nothing. They are a weight on our minds and uncertain, for they are never enjoyed without some anxiety or fear. Our happiness does not consist in the amount of things we possess,[2] for a modest amount is sufficient. Life on earth is a misery. The more spiritual we desire to become, the more bitter does this life seem to be, because we see and discover more clearly the defects and corruptions of human nature. To eat and drink, to wake and sleep, to rest and work and to be subject to the necessities of nature is a great trouble. It afflicts the devout, who would prefer to be released and set free from all sin.[3]

Our physical needs greatly hinder our spiritual life. So the Prophet prays to be set free from them, saying, 'Turn to me and be gracious to me, for I am lonely and afflicted.'[4] For it will be hard for those who fail to realize their own wretchedness, and harder still for those who love this wretched and transitory life.[5] For some cling so closely to this world that even by working and begging they can hardly earn the bare necessities. If it were possible they would be willing to remain here for ever, caring nothing for the Kingdom of God.

How mad and unfaithful are those who are so engrossed in earthly affairs that they care for nothing except material things.[6] These miserable people will ultimately know, to their great sorrow, that the things which they loved were vile and empty. But the Saints of God and all the devoted friends of Christ took little notice of either bodily pleasures or worldly prosperity, because all their hopes and desires were directed to the good things which are eternal.[7] All their desires lifted them up to eternal and invisible things, so that the love of visible things could not drag them down. Do not lose confidence in the progress of the spiritual life.[8] There is still time and opportunity.

Why postpone your good resolutions? Rise and start this very instant and say, 'Now is the acceptable time, now is the day of salvation.'[9] The time to achieve excellence is when things are going badly and you are in trouble. You must pass through fire and water before you can enter into the place of rest.[10] You will only overcome your depravity if you discipline yourself severely. As long as we live in a human body, we are bound to know sin and live with great weariness and sorrow. We would gladly be free of all troubles; but as we have lost our innocence through sin, we have also lost real happiness. We must therefore have endurance[11] and wait for God's mercy, until this wickedness passes away and death is swallowed up in life.[12]

Our frailty is very great because we are ever prone to evil.[13] Today you confess your sins; tomorrow you again commit the very sins you have confessed! Now you resolve to guard against them, and within an hour you succumb, as if you had not made any resolution! So considering our weakness and instability, it is right that we should humble ourselves and never be self-righteous. Through carelessness we can easily lose the progress that we had so earnestly won by God's grace.[14]

What state will we be left in, if our enthusiasm vanishes so quickly? Our fate will be very unhappy, if we decide to take some time off as though we had already reached the haven of peace and security,[15] when there is no vestige of holiness in our lives. It would be better to be instructed in the paths of a good life all over again, like a faithful novice. Then there might be some hope for our future improvement and greater spiritual progress.

TWENTY-THREE

A meditation on death

Very shortly, the end of your life will be imminent, so reflect on the state of your soul. We are here today and gone tomorrow,[1] and when we are out of sight we are out of mind. Our hearts are sluggish and hard, and if we think only of the present, nothing is provided for the future. You should arrange every action and thought as if today were the day of your death. If you had a clear conscience, death would hold no terrors for you,[2] but it would be better to avoid sin than to escape death.[3] If you are unprepared to die today, will you be more ready tomorrow?[4] Tomorrow is uncertain, so how can you be sure of it? If we have put so little right, what use is a long life? Sadly, a long life tends to increase our sins rather than our virtues!

If only we could spend even one day really well! Many calculate the years since their conversion, but their lives show little sign of improvement. It is frightening to die; it is even more perilous to live a long life. Blessed are those who keep in mind and prepare for the hour of their death. If you have ever witnessed someone's death remember that you also must go the same way.[5]

Every morning remember that you may not live until the evening. In the evening do not presume that you will see another day. Be ready at all times[6] and live so that death may never find you unprepared. Many die suddenly and unexpectedly; for the Son of Man will come at the time that you least expect Him.[7] When your final hour comes, you will begin to think very differently about your past life, and deeply regret that you have been so careless and remiss.

It is a very wise and happy person who tries to live life in such a way as they expect to be found in death. The following

attitudes will ensure a happy death: utter contempt for the
world; a strong desire to grow in holiness; a love of discipline;
the practice of penance; willing obedience; self-denial; accepting every trial for the love of Christ. While you enjoy health,
you can do much good; but when sickness comes you can do
little. Not many are made better through sickness and those
who go on frequent pilgrimages rarely find that it increases
their sanctification.[8]

Do not rely on friends and neighbours, and do not postpone
the salvation of your soul to a future date; for you will be forgotten more quickly than you think. It is better to make proper
provision and to gain favour than to depend on the help of
others. And if you make no provision for your own soul, who
will care for you in the future? The present moment is very precious. Now is the hour of favour; now is the day of salvation.[9]
It is very sad that you do not employ your time better when you
could win eternal life. The time will come when you will long
for even one day or one hour in which to repent; and who
knows whether you will find it?

Dear soul, from what peril and fear you could free yourself,
if you lived in holy fear, conscious of your death? Commit
yourself so to live now, that when you die you will be happy
and unafraid. Learn to die to the world so that you may live
with Christ.[10] Learn to despise all earthly things so that you
may freely go to Christ. Suppress your body now through penance so that you may enjoy a certain hope of salvation.

It is foolish to promise yourself a long life when you are not
sure about a single day.[11] How many have deceived themselves
and been snatched away unexpectedly? You have often heard
how someone was killed by the sword; another was drowned;
another fell from a height and had a broken neck; how another
died during a meal; another died while playing a game. Someone dies in a fire, another by the sword, another from disease,
another at the hands of robbers. Death is the end of us all[12] and
our days are like a fleeting shadow.[13]

Who will remember you when you are dead? Who will pray
for you? Act now, dear soul, do all you can; for you know neither the hour of your death nor how you will die. Gather the

riches of everlasting life while you have time.[14] Think only of your salvation and care for the things of God. Now is the time to make friends by honouring the Saints of God and by following their examples, so that when life is over they may welcome you into your eternal home.[15]

Remain as a stranger and pilgrim on this earth.[16] Do not be concerned with the things of this world. Keep your heart free and lift yourself up to God, for here you have no lasting city.[17] Direct your prayer and longings to heaven every day, so that at your death your soul may be free to pass joyfully into the presence of God.

TWENTY-FOUR

On judgement and the punishment of sinners

Always keep in mind your final end and how you will stand before the just Judge.[1] Nothing is hidden from Him and He cannot be influenced by bribes or excuses and is completely just.[2] O wretched and stupid sinner, you tremble before the anger of others, how will you answer to God[3] who knows all your evil ways? Why do you not prepare yourself for the Day of Judgement, when no one can defend you or excuse you? Then everyone will have to answer for themselves. While you live, your work is beneficial and your tears acceptable because sorrow cleanses the soul and makes peace with God.

A patient person goes through a healthy purgation. While suffering injuries, such a person is more concerned with the faults of others than their own wrongs and gladly prays for their enemies and forgives their offences. There is no delay in seeking pardon from others and they move more quickly to compassion than to anger. Such people have self-discipline and try to put the body under the spirit in every way. It is better to purge our sins and overcome our vices now than to save them up for future purgation. We can deceive ourselves by excessive love of the flesh.

The flames of hell have only our sins to feed on. The more you spare yourself now and indulge carnal pleasures, the more severe will be your ultimate punishment and the more fuel there will be for the flames. The pattern of our sins will be reflected in our punishment.[4]

Then the indolent will be prodded by fiery goads, and the gluttonous tormented by severe hunger and thirst.

Then the luxurious and pleasure-seeking will be plunged

into burning pitch and stinking sulphur while the envious will howl like angry dogs.

Every vice will receive appropriate retribution. The proud will be subjected to deep humiliation, and the greedy will experience misery and starvation.

An hour's punishment then will be more severe than a century of penance on earth. Here, we may often enjoy a rest from our work and the comfort of our friends, but thereafter there will be neither rest nor comfort for the damned. So live well now and grieve for your sins, so that on the Day of Judgement you may stand safely in the company of the blessed.

Then the just will be full of assurance to confront those who have oppressed them and made light of their sufferings.[5]

Then those who have humbly submitted to the judgement of others will judge others.

Then the poor and humble will have confidence, while the proud will be surrounded by fears on every side.

Then it will be revealed that those who have learned to be despised and fools for Christ's sake in this world were in fact wise.[6]

Then the devout will be happy and the ungodly will be sorry.

Then those who have patiently borne every trial will be glad and the mouths of the wicked will be silenced.[7]

Then those who disciplined their bodies will have greater joy than those who greatly indulged themselves.[8]

Then the ragged clothes of the poor will look splendid and those in gorgeous clothes will look drab.

Then the humble cottage of the poor will seem more desirable than a golden palace.

Then will a patient life be of more value than worldly power.

Then will humble obedience be raised up above the scheming and cunning.

Then a good, clean conscience will bring more joy than learned philosophy.

Then will contempt for riches be more valuable than all worldly treasures.

Then will devout prayer produce more pleasure than fine food.

Then those who have kept silence will be happier than those who gossip.

Then good deeds will be better than fine words.

Then will a disciplined life and deep penance prove to be more valuable than all worldly indulgence.

Learn to suffer a little now, so that you may be spared much worse troubles. Prove here what you can suffer hereafter. If you can put up with very little now, how will you endure the pains of hell? No one can enjoy both kinds of happiness: you cannot enjoy all the pleasures of this life and also reign with Christ in heaven. If you had enjoyed all the honours and pleasures of life here, how would that benefit you if you were to die now? All is vanity except to love God and serve God alone. For those who love God with all their hearts will not fear death, punishment, judgement or hell. For we gain access to God only through perfect love.[9] But if you continue to enjoy wickedness, it is not surprising if you fear death and judgement. However, if the love of God does not hold you back at least the fear of hell might restrain you. Those who put aside the fear of God cannot, for long, live a good life and will rapidly fall into the hands of the Devil.

TWENTY-FIVE

On our enthusiasm to amend our lives

Be alert[1] and persistent in the service of God, and frequently consider why you are here and why you have renounced the world. It was so that you could live with God and have a spiritual life. So work hard to make progress, and you will soon receive a reward for your endeavours. Then you will not be troubled by fear or sorrow. Work hard for a brief time now and you will find rest for your soul and everlasting joy. If you remain faithful in all you do, you can be sure that God will be faithful and be generous in rewarding you.[2] Keep a firm hope that you will receive the victor's crown,[3] but do not be over-confident lest you become smug and self-satisfied.

There was once a man[4] who was very anxious and dithered between hope and fear. One day, when overcome with despair, he lay prostrate in prayer before the altar in church and, pondering these matters in his mind, said: 'Oh, if only I knew that I would always persevere!' Then he heard in his heart a reply from God: 'If you knew this what would you do? Do now what you would do then, and all will be well.' So, having been comforted and strengthened, he committed himself to the will of God. His restless anxiety went away, and he no longer wished to ask what would happen to him, but strove eagerly to learn the perfect and acceptable will of God.[5] So he was equipped for good work of every kind.[6]

'Trust in the Lord, and do good,' says the Prophet, 'so you will live in the land, and enjoy security.'[7] One thing that deters people from their spiritual journey and enthusiastic correction is the fear of great difficulties and the cost of victory. But be assured that those who grow in virtue more than their companions are those who fight manfully to triumph over whatever is most

difficult and distasteful. The more completely we overcome
and cleanse ourselves in the spirit, the more we gain and deserve
overflowing grace.

We do not all have the same things to overcome, but whatever strong passions we have to subdue, those who are diligent
and committed will certainly make greater progress than those
who are naturally self-controlled but less committed to spirituality. The two main things which assist the amendment of life
are a forcible withdrawal from the vices to which we naturally
incline, and a determined pursuit of any grace that we especially need. In particular, try to avoid and overcome those
things that you dislike in other people.

Seek to advance in everything, imitate any examples that you
see or hear and inspire you. But if you notice anything blameworthy, take care to avoid doing the same yourself. And if you
ever fail to do so, correct your behaviour straight away. As you
observe others, so others observe you.[8] How good and pleasant
it is to see enthusiastic and devout members of the community
keeping good manners and discipline.[9] And how sad and painful
it is to see those who are disorderly and fail to live up to their calling. It is very harmful if people neglect the real purpose of their
vocation and turn to matters which are not their real concern.

Remember that your avowed purpose is to keep before you the
likeness of Christ crucified.[10] As you meditate on the life of Christ
you should feel sorry that you have not tried hard enough to conform yourself to Him, even though you have spent a long time as
God's disciple. A Religious who earnestly and devoutly contem-
plates the most holy life and Passion of our Lord will find in it
everything profitable and needful. Nor would any Religious seek
any other model than Jesus.[11] If only Christ crucified would come
into our hearts, how quickly and fully we would be instructed!

A zealous Religious readily accepts and obeys all orders. But
a careless and lukewarm Religious has trouble after trouble
and, lacking real inward consolation, finds sorrow on every
side and is forbidden to seek exterior support. Religious who
disregard the Rule are exposed to dreadful ruin. Those who
desire an easier and undisciplined life will always be unstable,
because one thing or another around them will be displeasing.

Examine how many of those who live under strict discipline behave. They rarely go out, they live a secluded life; they eat the dullest food; they work hard; they talk little; they keep long vigils; they rise early; they spend a lot of time in prayer; they study regularly and control themselves with discipline.

Think about the Carthusians, the Cistercians and the monks and nuns of the various Orders,[12] how they rise during the night to sing praises to our Lord. If you were slothful it would shame you when such a great company of Religious are singing the praises of God.

Would that all we could do was to offer endless praise to the Lord our God with our heart and voice! If you had no need of food, drink or rest you could praise God without ceasing[13] and give yourself wholly to spiritual matters. This would make you far happier than you are when compelled to serve your bodily needs. If only those needs did not exist, then we might enjoy the spiritual feasts of the soul which alas we so rarely taste.

When we no longer seek human comfort from anyone then we begin to enjoy God perfectly and we will be content whatever comes to us. Then we will not rejoice in owning a great deal, or feel sorry for having nothing, but will simply commit ourselves to be faithful to God who is All in All.[14] In God nothing passes away or dies, for all things live for Him and fulfil His will continually.[15]

Always remember your end[16] and that lost time never returns. You will only acquire virtue with care and diligence. If you begin to be careless everything will go wrong for you. But if you give yourself to prayer, you will find great peace and your work will grow lighter by the help of God's grace and your love of virtue. Those who are enthusiastic and sincere are ready for anything. The war against our vices and passions is harder than any physical work. Whoever fails to overcome smaller faults will find them being replaced, little by little, by larger ones.[17] If you have spent the day well, your evenings will always be peaceful. Watch yourself, lift yourself up, discipline yourself and, whatever the action of others, do not neglect your own soul. The stricter you are with yourself, the greater is your spiritual progress.

PART TWO

THE CHAPTERS OF
BOOK TWO

Here begins the advice on
living the inner life

ONE

On the inner life

'The Kingdom of God is among you,'[1] says our Lord. 'Return
to Me with all your heart.'[2] Reject this sad world 'and you will
find rest for your souls'.[3] Learn to turn from worldly things and
devote yourself to spiritual things, and you will see the Kingdom of God come within you. For the Kingdom of God is
'peace and joy in the Holy Spirit'.[4] These things are not granted
to wicked people. Christ will come to you[5] and will offer you
His consolations, if you prepare a place for Him in your heart.
All true glory and beauty lies within[6] and He likes to dwell
there. He frequently visits those with an inner life and offers
sweet conversation, consoling grace, considerable peace, and
friendship which will exceed all expectation.

So come faithful soul, and prepare your heart for your divine
spouse that He may be willing to come and dwell with you.[7]
For He says, 'Those who love Me will keep My Word; and My
Father will love them, and We will come to them and make Our
home with them.'[8] So welcome Christ and forbid entry to
others.[9] When Christ is with you, you are very rich, and He will
take care of you in every way, so that you will not need to
depend on others. People are erratic and will let you down; but
Christ stands for ever[10] and is a resolute companion to the end.

Never put your complete trust and reliance in frail and mortal people, however helpful and valuable they may be to you.
Nor, if sometimes others oppose and contradict you, should
you feel very sorry for yourself. Those who support you today
may oppose you tomorrow; for people are as changeable as
the weather. Put your complete trust in the Lord,[11] direct your

reverence and love to Him alone. He will defend you and will establish all things for the best. Here you have no lasting city[12] and everywhere you are a stranger and an alien.[13] You will never have peace unless you are inwardly united with Christ.

What do you seek here, since this is not your final resting place? So remember that all things in this world are passing away and that your true home is in heaven.[14] All things are transient, and you are passing with them. Take care that you do not cling to them, in case you become trapped and perish with them. Let all your thoughts be with the Most High and focus your humble praying on Christ without ceasing.[15] If it is hard to contemplate high and heavenly things, take rest in the Passion of Christ, and love to hide in His sacred wounds.[16] For if you devoutly seek the stigmata of Jesus[17] and the precious marks of His Passion, you will find great strength in your troubles. And, if you are despised, you will not be bothered, because you will have little interest in the words of your detractors.

Christ our Lord was despised by many, and in His hour of need was abandoned to the insults of His enemies by His followers and friends. Christ was willing to suffer and to be despised.[18] So why do you complain? Christ had enemies and slanderers; do you expect everyone to be your friends and benefactors? How will your patience be rewarded if you are not willing to endure suffering? If you wish to reign with Christ, you will have to suffer with Christ and for Christ.[19]

If you had entered fully into the mind of Christ and tasted something of His burning love, you would care nothing for your own success or failure. For the love of Jesus causes us to regard ourselves very humbly. The honest inward lovers of Jesus and the truth are free from disorderly feelings and can easily turn to God. They rise above themselves and rest happily in God.

How very wise are those who realize the true value of things, and not as they are said or reputed to be. For our knowledge comes from God[20] and not from man. Those who walk by inner insight, and are not unduly influenced by outward things, need no special time or place for prayer. Those with an inner life easily find recollection, since they are never totally involved in outward affairs. So our outward occupations and necessary tasks do not distract us, and we adapt ourselves to whatever crops up. Those with a well-ordered and focused inner life are not disturbed by the strange and perverse ways of others. For we are only hindered and distracted by such things if we allow them to dominate us.

If you had a well-disciplined inner life and a pure heart all things would turn to your benefit and advantage.[21] But because we are not fully dead to ourselves, nor detached from all worldly things, we are often confused and offended. Nothing defiles and entraps us more than a selfish love of material things. If you rejected all outward comfort you would be able to contemplate heavenly things and experience greater inner happiness.

TWO

On humble submission to God

Do not be greatly concerned about who is for you or who is against you, but prepare and work to have God on your side in all that you do.[1] Keep a good conscience, and God will mightily defend you; for whoever enjoys the protection of God cannot be harmed by human malice. If you learn to suffer in silence, you will be sure of receiving God's comfort.[2] God knows the times and the means to save you, so put your complete trust in Him. God is strong to help you[3] and to free you from all disturbances. It is salutary for us that others know and can reveal our faults, for it will keep us humble.

When we humbly admit our failings, we can quickly appease anger and be reconciled with anyone we have offended. God protects and liberates humble people. He loves and consoles them. He bends down and gives great grace to the humble.[4] He lifts them from depression to glory. He reveals His secrets to the humble. He calls them and draws them to Himself. Even in the middle of trouble, humble people remain wholly at peace. They trust in God and not in worldly things. You cannot think that you have made any spiritual progress unless you consider yourself the least of all.

THREE

On being good and peaceful

Firstly, be at peace with yourself and then you will be able to offer peace to others. Peaceful people do more good than learned ones. An impulsive person may even turn good into evil and readily listens to evil; but those who are good and peaceable turn everything to good. Those who are really at peace do not think evil of anyone; but those who are discontented and restless are tormented by many suspicions. Having no peace in themselves, they will not allow others any peace. They frequently say what they should not say, and fail to do what they ought to do. They are aware of their neighbours' duties, but indifferent to their own. So first look after your own affairs; then you may properly be concerned for your neighbours.

You easily excuse and explain your own activities, but you will not accept the explanations of others. It would be better to accuse yourself and to excuse your neighbours. If you want others to bear your burdens, you must put up with theirs.[1] Realize how far you are from the love and humility which expresses no anger or indignation except to yourself. It is no great thing to keep company with the good and the gentle, for this is naturally pleasing to us all. All of us enjoy living in peace and prefer those who are like-minded. But living peacefully among rough, obstinate and ill-disciplined people and those who disagree with us is a great grace and a highly commendable human virtue.

There are some who can remain at peace with themselves and with everyone else.[2] There are some who have no peace with themselves, nor allow others to be at peace. There are others who are at peace with themselves and try to lead others into peace. Our peace in this present life should not depend on absence of adversity but on humble acceptance. Those who accept suffering will enjoy peace. Such a person is a conqueror of the self, a ruler of the world, a friend of Christ and an inheritor of heaven.[3]

FOUR

On purity of mind and simplicity of purpose

There are two wings that lift us up above earthly things. They are simplicity and purity. Simplicity inspires our motivation and purity inspires our devotion. Simplicity reaches after God; purity discovers and enjoys Him. You will not find any obstacle to good deeds if you are inwardly free from uncontrolled desires. If you are free from uncontrolled desires and seek only the will of God and the good of your neighbour, you will enjoy inner freedom. If your heart is right, everything in the world will be a mirror reflecting eternity and a book of holy instruction. For there is nothing created, however small and insignificant, that is not a reflection of the goodness of God.

If you were inwardly good and pure, you would see and understand all things clearly and easily. A pure heart permeates both heaven and hell. We judge outward things in accordance with our inner nature. It is the pure in heart who will possess any joy that there is in this world.[1] The evil heart is most likely to experience all sorts of trouble or distress.[2] In the same way as iron plunged into the furnace loses its rust and becomes bright and shiny, so those who turn totally to God lose their sloth and become transformed into new creatures.[3]

When someone begins to grow lazy and lukewarm in spirit, even the slightest piece of work seems frightening and they welcome any outward comfort. But when we overcome ourselves and move boldly towards God, then we will dismiss as nothing our endeavours, which we previously found very burdensome.

FIVE

On self-knowledge

It is not possible to trust in ourselves, because we often lack grace and common sense. Through carelessness we can easily lose the few insights we have. We often do not realize how blind we are. We often commit evil and we make it worse by excusing ourselves. Sometimes we are stirred by emotion and mistake it for devotion. We condemn small faults in others, but we overlook worse faults in ourselves.[1] We are too quick to resent and feel what we suffer from others, but we fail to consider how much others suffer from us. Those who consider their own faults openly and honestly will find no reason to judge others harshly.

The spiritual person puts the care of the soul above everything else,[2] and those who carefully look after their own affairs are prepared to be silent about other people. You will never become spiritual and devout unless you concentrate on your own soul and stop criticizing others. If you concentrate totally on God and your soul you will be less affected by external events.[3] Where are you when you fail to look after yourself? And what have you gained if you have neglected your soul and become preoccupied by many matters?[4] If you desire real peace and union with God, concentrate on yourself and put everything else aside.

Keep free from the snares of the world and you will make good progress; but if you put great value on worldly matters, this will become a real obstacle. Let nothing noble, pleasant or desirable replace whatever comes from God and serving God alone. Regard all creaturely concerns as empty comfort. The soul that loves God considers anything other than God as worthless. God alone is eternal and infinitely great, and He fills all things.[5] He alone is the real comfort of the soul and the joy of the heart.

SIX

On the satisfaction of a clear conscience

The glory of a good person is revealed in a good conscience.[1] Keep a quiet conscience and you will always be happy. A quiet conscience will tolerate a lot and remain joyful in all troubles,[2] but an evil conscience is always fearful and uneasy. You will be at ease if your heart does not reproach you, and you are happy only when you have done right. Wicked people never know real happiness, nor do they enjoy inward peace, for 'There is no peace for the wicked', says the Lord.[3] Although they say, 'We are at peace; no evil can happen to us, and no one will dare to harm us', God's anger will rise up suddenly. Then all their works will come to nothing and their plans will perish.

Those who truly love God do not find it hard to glory in suffering, for in this way they rejoice in the glory of the Cross of our Lord.[4] The splendour that is given to us and received by humanity is short-lived and sorrow is always its companion. The praise of good people lies in their own conscience, not in the praise of others. For the joy of the Saints comes from God and is in God, and their joy is in the truth.[5] Whoever wants true and lasting glory cares nothing for the splendours of the world. Whoever desires worldly splendour, and does not actually despise it, reveals that they have little love for the glory of heaven. Great tranquillity of the heart belongs to those who are indifferent to both praise and blame.

Those who have a clear conscience can be easily content and at peace. Receiving public acclamation does not make you holy, and you are none the worse for being blamed. You are just as you are, and you cannot be considered any greater than you are in the sight of God. If you know your interior self, you will not mind what other people say about you. For, while the world considers the outward appearance, God only looks into our hearts. Others may see your actions but God knows your motives. The sign of the humble soul is always to be doing good and to think little of oneself. It is a sign of great purity and inward faith to desire no human consolation.

When people seek no outside witness for support, this is a demonstration that their whole trust is in God. 'For', as St Paul says, 'it is not those who commend themselves that are approved, but those whom the Lord commends.'[6] To live inwardly for God and not to be bound by worldly affections is the proper state of the devout person.

SEVEN

On loving Jesus above everything

Blessed are those who understand what it is to love Jesus and despise oneself for His sake. You must surrender all other love in order to love Him, for Jesus demands our love above everything else. It is a vain deception to love all created things. Loving Jesus is more faithful and enduring. Those who cling to worldly things will fall when they fail. But those who cling to Jesus will stand firm for ever. So love Him and keep Him as your friend. When everyone else deserts you, He will not abandon you, nor permit you to perish in the end. Finally, whether you want it or not, you will be parted from all living things.

Cling to Jesus in life and in death and commit yourself to His faithfulness. When everyone else fails you, He alone can help you. The characteristic of your Beloved is that He will not share His love for you with another. He wants your heart for Himself alone, and to reign there as a king on His throne. If it were possible for you to empty your heart of all creatures, Jesus would enjoy living with you.[1] The trust you put in people other than Jesus is almost completely wasted. Do not trust or lean on a reed swaying in the wind,[2] for 'All people are grass, their constancy is like the flower of the field.'[3]

If you only look at someone's outward appearance, you will often be deceived. For if you seek comfort or gain from others, you will frequently be disappointed. If you seek Jesus in everything you will undoubtedly find Jesus. And if you seek yourself, you will certainly find yourself, and that will be your loss. Anyone who does not seek Jesus causes greater self-harm than the entire world and all enemies could ever do.

EIGHT

On having Jesus as an intimate friend

When Jesus is with us, all is well and nothing seems difficult; but when Jesus is absent, everything is hard. When Jesus does not speak to our hearts, all other consolation is empty, but if Jesus speaks even a single word, we are greatly comforted. Did not Mary Magdalene rise at once from the place where she wept when Martha said, 'The Teacher is here and is calling for you'?[1] What a happy moment when Jesus calls us from our weeping to the joy of the spirit! How dry and hard of heart you are without Jesus. How stupid and pointless if you desire anything other than Jesus. It is a greater injury to you than losing the whole world.

What could the world offer you without Jesus? It is actually hell to be without Jesus. To be with Jesus is to know the sweetness of heaven. If Jesus is with you, no enemy can harm you. Whoever finds Jesus finds rich treasure and good above every good. Anyone who loses Jesus loses too much, more than the whole world. Those who live without Jesus are real paupers and those who stand in Jesus' favour are like millionaires.

It is a great art to know how to converse with Jesus. It is great wisdom to know how to hold on to Jesus. If you are humble and at peace, Jesus will abide with you. If you turn aside to worldly things, you will soon cause Jesus to leave you and you will lose His favour. If you send Him away and lose Him, with whom can you take refuge and whom may you seek to be your friend? Without a friend it is not possible to live happily. If Jesus is not your best friend you will be very sad and lonely, so it is foolish to trust or rejoice in anyone else. It is better to be at enmity with the whole world than to offend Jesus. So, of all your dear friends, ensure that Jesus is loved first, and above all others.

Love everyone for Jesus' sake, but love Jesus for His own sake. Jesus Christ alone is to be loved with a special love, for He alone is the best and most faithful of friends. In Him and for His sake, love both friend and enemy, and pray to Him for all of them, in order that everyone may know and love Him. Do not desire to become the object of special praise or love, for that is due to God alone; for no one is like Him. Do not desire that the total love of anyone should be given just to you and do not give your heart to anyone; rather let Jesus abide in you[2] and in every good person.

Inwardly be pure and free, unentangled with any created thing. If you wish to be free, offer a pure and spotless heart to Jesus and see how gracious the Lord is.[3] You will only achieve this if His grace calls and guides you. Once you have thrown aside and forgotten everything else, you can be united with Him alone. When the grace of God comes to us, we are strong in everything; but when it departs we are left poor and weak and we feel abandoned to punishment and sorrow. When this happens to you, do not despair or be discouraged. Accept God's will calmly, bearing all that comes to you for the glory of Christ. For after winter comes summer and fair weather comes after a storm.[4]

NINE

On lacking all comfort

When we enjoy the comfort of God it is not difficult to despise human comforts. It is a great thing to be able to reject all consolation, human or divine, and willingly to suffer desolation of the heart for God's sake and not to seek anything for yourself or any personal merit. Is it any proof of virtue that you are filled with joy and devotion when God sends His grace? Surely everyone longs for this, for those who are carried by God's grace can travel easily. It is no surprise, when Almighty God carries us along, that we do not feel weary, and we are led by the greatest of all leaders.[1]

We enjoy much comfort and it is only with difficulty that our self-love is removed. Think how the holy martyr Laurence, with the priest he served,[2] triumphed over the world because he despised all that seemed enjoyable. Through the love of Christ he allowed God's high priest Sixtus, whom he greatly loved, to be taken from him. So, through the love of his Creator, he conquered his love for humanity and preferred the will of God to all human comfort. So you must learn to surrender even your closest and best friend for the love of God. And do not grieve when a friend leaves you, for in the end we will all be parted from each other.

To learn how to master ourselves and direct all our love to God fully, we have to struggle for a long, hard time. When we rely on ourselves, we easily come to rely on human consolation as well. But the true lover of Christ and the keen seeker after holiness does not fall back on these things or look for pleasurable sensations. They prefer to endure hard work and great tribulations for Christ's sake.

When God bestows spiritual consolation accept it with a

grateful heart; but remember that it comes as a free gift from God and not because you deserve it. Do not be proud, or over-joyful, or stupid or presumptuous. It is better to accept the gift humbly and to be more careful and wise in all that you do. For this hour will pass and temptation will follow it. When consolation is withdrawn, do not immediately despair. But wait for the will of heaven, humbly and patiently, for God is able to restore to you an even richer consolation than before. Those who know the ways of God will not find this new or strange, for the great Saints and Prophets of old often experienced such changes.

When grace was with him David exclaimed, 'I said in my prosperity "I shall never be moved."'[3] But when grace was taken away and he described his experience, he added, 'You hid Your face; I was dismayed.'[4] Yet in his trouble he does not despair; he prays to the Lord more earnestly: 'To You, O Lord, I will cry, and to the Lord I will make supplication.'[5] At last he received the answer to his prayer and declared, 'The Lord has heard, and been gracious to me! The Lord has become my helper!'[6] But in what way? 'You have turned my mourning into dancing,' he said; 'You have taken off my sackcloth and clothed me with joy.'[7] 'If this is the experience of great Saints, it is not for us, poor and frail as we are, to despair if we are sometimes devout and sometimes lukewarm. The Spirit comes and goes as He sees fit; and so Job says, 'You visit them every morning, test them every moment.'[8]

Then in what can I place my hope or trust except in the great mercy of God alone, and in the hope of His heavenly grace?[9] For if I can enjoy human company, or devout Religious or faithful friends; whether holy books, excellent treatises, or delightful singing and hymns – all these are of little help or comfort when I am without grace and left in a poor state. When this happens the best remedy is patience and submission to the will of God.

I have never found anyone, be it a Religious or a devout person, who has not sometimes experienced a withdrawal of grace or felt a loss of devotion. And no Saint has ever lived, however entranced and enlightened, who did not suffer temptation sooner or later. For those who have never suffered some trials for God's sake are not worthy of the heavenly contemplation. In fact, the temptation that comes first is usually a sign of comfort to follow. For heavenly comfort is promised to those who have been tried and tempted. 'To everyone who is courageous I will give permission to eat from the tree of life,' says God.[10]

Divine consolation is granted that we may be stronger to endure adversity, and temptation follows so that we may not be proud of our virtue. The Devil never sleeps,[11] nor has the flesh died.[12] So never stop preparing yourself for the battle against unrelenting enemies who are ready to ambush you on every side.

TEN

On gratitude for God's grace

You were born to work, so why do you look for rest? Commit yourself to suffering rather than comfort and to carrying the Cross rather than happiness. What worldly person would not rather gladly receive spiritual comfort and joy, if they were sure of keeping it? For spiritual consolation exceeds all earthly delights and joys of the flesh. All worldly pleasures are either futile or shameful; only spiritual joys are pleasant and delightful, for they are born of virtue and God infuses them into the pure of heart.[1] But no one may enjoy these divine consolations because they want to, for temptation is never far away.

Excessive self-confidence and a false sense of freedom are great obstacles to heavenly visitations. God is generous in giving us the grace of comfort, but we do badly by not returning everything to God in grateful thanks. The reason why God's graces cannot flow freely in us is that we are ungrateful to the giver and do not return them to their fount and source. God will always give grace to those who are grateful, but what He gives to the humble is withheld from the proud.

I do not want any consolation that would deny me penitence, nor do I aspire to any contemplation which might make me proud. All that is high is not holy, nor is all that is pleasant good. Every desire is not pure, nor is all that we value pleasing to God. I would prefer gladly to accept the sort of grace which makes me increasingly humble and devout, and the more willing to renounce myself. For those who are taught by the gift of grace and reproved by its removal will not attribute any good to themselves, but will acknowledge real poverty and a lack of virtue. 'Give to God the things that are God's.'[2] Attribute to yourself whatever is yours. So then give thanks to God for His grace and realize that the guilt and penalty of sin belong only to you.

Always put yourself in the lowest place[3] and you will be awarded the highest; for the highest cannot stand without the lowest. The Saints stand the highest in God's sight and are lowest in their own eyes. The more glorious they are, the more humble is their spirit.

Filled with truth and heavenly glory, they have no desire for heavenly glory. Rooted and grounded in God, they cannot be proud. They ascribe all goodness to God. They do not look for glory from each other but only the glory which comes from God.[4] Their desire and longing is that God will be praised above all things in their lives, and in the lives of all His Saints.

Be grateful for the smallest blessing, and you will deserve to receive greater. The smallest gifts are to be valued the same as the greatest, and simple grace as a special favour. If you recall the dignity of Him who gives, you will not consider any gift to be small or mean; for nothing that is given by the Most High God can be without value. Even if He gives us punishment and pain, we should accept them gladly, for everything He allows to happen to us is always for our salvation. Whoever wants to retain the favour of God must be thankful for God's grace, and be patient when it is taken away. Let us pray for its return; let us be wise and humble for fear of losing it.

ELEVEN

On the lack of lovers of the Cross

Jesus has many who love His Kingdom of Heaven, but few who will carry His Cross.[1] He has many who desire comfort, but few who desire suffering. He finds many to share His feasts, but few His fasting. Many want to rejoice with Him, but few will stay by Him. Many follow Jesus to the breaking of bread, but few will drink the cup of His suffering. Many admire His miracles, but few follow Him to the ignominy of the Cross. Many love Jesus as long as no hardship touches them. Many praise and bless Him as long as they are receiving comfort from Him. But if Jesus withdraws Himself from them, they fall into complaining and great dejection.

Those who love Jesus for His own sake and not for the sake of selfish comfort will praise Him in every trial and anguish of heart, no less than in great joy. And they would praise Him and give Him thanks, even if He never offered them any comfort.

How powerful is the pure love of Jesus, which is free from self-love and self-interest. Those who are seeking comfort like capitalists betray themselves as being lovers of themselves, rather than of Christ. They are always thinking about personal gain and satisfaction. Where is the person who is willing to serve God without any rewards?[2]

There are not many who are so spiritual that they can be totally stripped of self-love. Who can point to someone who is utterly poor in spirit and detached from the world? 'His rare worth exceeds all on earth.'[3] If someone gives away all their possessions, it is nothing. If someone undergoes severe penance, it is very little. If someone attains great knowledge, it is only a small step. If someone has great virtue and the most ardent devotion, much is still lacking and especially the 'one thing necessary'.[4] What is that? That we leave ourselves and everything else and totally deny ourselves, and retain no trace of self-love. And when we have done all that we ought to do, let us feel that we have done nothing.

Let us not consider important what others regard as important, but let us honestly confess that we are unprofitable servants. For these are the words of Truth Himself: 'When you have done all that you were ordered to do, say, "We are worthless slaves".'[5] Then we may be called poor and naked in spirit, and say with the Prophet, 'I am lonely and afflicted.'[6] Yet no one is richer, more powerful or more free than someone who has left self and everything else behind, to sit in the lowest place.[7]

TWELVE

On the royal road of the Holy Cross

'If any want to become My followers, let them deny themselves and take up their cross and follow Me.'[1] This saying of Jesus seems hard, but how much harder it will be to hear the severe words, 'You that are accursed, depart from me into the eternal fire'![2] For those who now freely hear and obey the message of the Cross[3] will not be frightened to hear the sentence of eternal damnation. When our Lord comes as Judge, the sign of the Cross will appear in the heavens.[4] Then all the servants of the Cross, who during their lives conformed themselves to the Crucified,[5] will stand with confidence before Christ their Judge.

Why then are you afraid to take up the Cross, which is the road to the Kingdom?

In the Cross is salvation

In the Cross is life

In the Cross is protection against our enemies

In the Cross you are immersed in heavenly sweetness

In the Cross is strength of mind

In the Cross is joy in the spirit

In the Cross is the fullness of virtue

In the Cross is perfect holiness

There is neither salvation of the soul nor hope of eternal life except in the Cross. Take up the Cross, therefore, and follow Jesus,[6] and go forward to eternal life.[7] Christ has gone before you, bearing His Cross.[8] He died for you on the Cross so that you might also carry your cross and desire to die on the Cross with Him. For if you die with Him, you will also live with Him,[9] and if you share His sufferings, you will also share His glory.

See how everything rests in the Cross and everything depends on dying. There is no other way to life and to real inner peace except the way of the Cross and daily self-denial. Walk where you will, seek what you will; you will find no better way above, nor safer way below, than the road of the Holy Cross. If you arrange and order all things to your own ideas and desires, you will still have to endure suffering, whether you want to or not. Thus you will always find the Cross. For you will either find physical pain, or suffer mental and spiritual trauma.

Sometimes God will withdraw from you, at other times you will be disturbed by your neighbour; and, even more, you will often be a pain to yourself. Nor will any remedy or consolation bring you relief, but you must put up with it as long as God wishes. For God wants you to experience tribulations without comfort so that you can fully surrender yourself to Him, and grow more humble through suffering. Those who suffer like Christ will feel in their hearts the Passion of Christ. The Cross stands ready and waiting for you everywhere.[10] You can't escape from it, wherever you go you take yourself with you and always find yourself. Look upwards or downwards, inwards or outwards and you will find the Cross everywhere. So, if you wish to attain inner peace and win the eternal crown, you must be patient in all things.

If you willingly carry the Cross, it will carry you and take you to your desired end, where pain shall be no more;[11] but it will not happen in this life. If you resent carrying the Cross, you will make it a burden and it will weigh you down heavily, but you must carry it. If you throw away one cross, you will without doubt find another, probably much heavier one.

Do you think you can avoid what every mortal being cannot escape? Which of the Saints lived without the Cross or trials? Even our Lord Jesus Christ was never without sorrow and pain as long as He lived. 'Was it not necessary that the Messiah should suffer these things,' He said, 'and then enter into His glory?'[12] Why then do you seek any other road than this Royal Road of the Holy Cross? The whole life of Christ was a cross and martyrdom; and do you look for rest and selfish pleasure?

You will be greatly mistaken, if you seek anything except to endure trials, for all this mortal life is full of trouble,[13] and everywhere marked with crosses. The further we advance in the spiritual life, the heavier and more frequently will we find crosses. For our ever-deepening love of God makes more bitter the sorrows of this life in exile.

Yet those who suffer in many ways do not lack solace and comfort, for they learn the great benefit to be gained from carrying the Cross. For while we carry it with goodwill, the whole weight is changed by the hope of God's consolation. The more the body is subdued by affliction, the more the soul is strengthened by interior grace. Sometimes we are greatly comforted by the desire to suffer adversity for the love of conforming to the Cross of Christ, so that we would not wish to be without pain and grief.[14] For we know that the more we can suffer for His sake the more pleasing we will be to God. This desire does not spring from our own strength but from the grace of Christ, which can and does achieve great things in frail humanity. So the things which nature fears and avoids, we can meet boldly and love through a fervent spirit.

We are not naturally inclined to carry the Cross, to love the Cross, to chastise and control our bodies;[15] to refuse honours, to accept insults with goodwill, to despise ourselves and welcome ridicule, to tolerate adversity and loss and to have no desire for prosperity in this world.

If you trust in your own strength, you will not be able to achieve any of these things. But if you trust in the Lord, you will be given heavenly strength, and the world and the flesh will be under your control. Nor will you fear your enemy the Devil if you are armed with faith and marked with the Cross of Christ.[16]

Therefore, as good and faithful servants of Christ, decide bravely to carry the Cross of your Lord, who was crucified for love of you. Prepare to endure many trials and obstacles in this vale of tears, for it will be your lot wherever you are. You will encounter them wherever you hide yourself. It is bound to be like this, nor is there any remedy or means of escape from ills and pains. You have to endure them. If you wish to be His friend and to share everything with Him, lovingly drink the cup of the Lord.[17] Let God offer the consolations that He wishes. But prepare yourself to endure trials, seeing them as the greatest of all comforts, for 'the sufferings of this present time are not worth comparing with the glory about to be revealed to us',[18] even if you were the only one to endure them all.

All will be well with you when you have come to that state where tribulation seems sweet and acceptable to you for Christ's sake, for you will have found heaven on earth. But as long as suffering is a pain to you and you try to escape from it, it will not be well for you, for the troubles you try to escape will follow you everywhere.

If you prepare yourself, as you must, to suffer and die, everything will be better for you and you will find peace. Even if, like St Paul, you were 'caught up into paradise',[19] you would not be safe from experiencing further adversity. For Jesus says, 'I myself will show him how much he must suffer for the sake of My name.'[20] So be prepared to suffer, if you wish to love Jesus and serve Him for ever.

If only you were worthy to suffer for the name of Jesus! What great and enduring a glory would be yours. How great would be the joy of the Saints of God! How pleased your friends would be. For we all approve of patience, but few are willing to suffer. As many people suffer such severe things for worldly reasons, it is only right that you should be prepared to suffer a little for Christ.

Remember that you must live a dying life. The more completely we die to self, the more we begin to live to God.[21] No one is fit to understand heavenly things unless we are willing to endure hardships for Christ's sake. Nothing is more acceptable to God and nothing is more salutary for you than to suffer gladly for Christ's sake. And if you have the choice, choose to suffer hardships for Christ's sake rather than be fortified by much compassion. For, in this way, you will resemble Christ and all His Saints. For our worth and spiritual progress does not consist in enjoying such sweetness and consolation, but rather in bearing heavy burdens and troubles.

If there had been a better way for the salvation of humanity other than suffering, Christ would have revealed it in His Word and His life. But He clearly urges both His own disciples and all who wish to follow Him to carry the Cross, saying, 'If any want to become My followers, let them deny themselves and take up their cross and follow Me.'[22] So when we have read and considered all things our resolve must be that 'It is through many persecutions that we must enter the Kingdom of God.'[23]

PART THREE

THE CHAPTERS OF
BOOK FOUR

Here begins a devout encouragement
to receive Holy Communion

The Voice of Christ

'Come to Me, all you that are weary and are carrying heavy burdens, and I will give you rest,'[1] says the Lord.

'The bread that I will give for the life of the world is My Flesh.'[2]

Take and eat; 'This is My Body, which is given for you. Do this in remembrance of Me.'[3]

'Those who eat My Flesh and drink My Blood abide in Me, and I in them.'[4]

'The words that I have spoken to you are spirit and life.'[5]

ONE

On how Christ should be received with great reverence

DISCIPLE: O Christ, the everlasting Truth, these are Your own words even though they were not spoken at one time or one place. And as they are Your true words, I must accept them with gratitude and trust. These are Your words and You have spoken them; they are mine, because You have given them to me for my salvation. I received them willingly from Your lips, so that they may be more deeply imprinted on my heart. Your words so tender, so full of sweetness and love, give me courage; but I am appalled by my own sins and my sinful conscience holds me back from these great mysteries.

You command me to approach You in faith, if I wish to share with You and receive the everlasting food in order to gain eternal life and glory. 'Come to Me,' You say, 'all you that are weary and are carrying heavy burdens, and I will give you rest.'[1] O Lord my God, how sweet and loving are these words in the ears of a sinner, with which You invite the poor and needy to the Communion of Your most holy Body! But who am I, O Lord, that I should presume to approach You? The heaven of heavens cannot contain You[2] and yet You say, 'All of you come to Me.'

What is the meaning of this loving invitation? How can I dare to come when I am unaware of any good in me on which I may presume? How can I, who have so often done evil in Your sight,[3] invite You into my house? Angels and Archangels reverence You. The Saints and the Justified stand in awe of You. Yet You say, 'All of you come to Me.' No one would believe it to be true unless You said it. And, unless You gave the command, no one would dare to approach.

Noah, who was a good man,[4] is said to have worked for a hundred years to build the ark, so that he and a few others could be saved.[5] So how can I prepare myself in a brief hour to receive with great devotion the Creator of the world? Your great servant and chosen friend Moses constructed an Ark of indestructible wood[6] and overlaid it with the purest gold in order to contain the Tablets of the Law. So how can I, a miserable creature, so lightly dare to receive You, the giver of life and the author of the law? Solomon, the wisest king of Israel,[7] spent seven years building a magnificent temple in praise of Your name. For eight days he celebrated the feast of its dedication and provided a thousand peace offerings. To the sound of trumpets, he solemnly and joyfully carried the Ark of the Covenant to its appointed place. Then how can I, the most unworthy and poorest of people, welcome You into my house[8] when I can hardly spend half an hour in devotion? If only I could spend half an hour as I should!

O my God, how earnestly all these people sought to please You! And alas how little I can do! What a short time I spend preparing myself for Communion! I am rarely completely recollected and very seldom free from distractions. No improper thoughts should enter my mind in Your divine saving presence, for it is not an Angel but the Lord of Angels who comes to be my guest.

What a difference there is between the Ark of the Covenant and its artefacts,[9] and Your sacred Body with its inexpressible virtues; between the sacrifices of the old law which foreshadowed the sacrifice to come, and the true victim of Your Body, which completes the old sacrifices.

Then why am I not more ablaze at Your adorable presence? Why do I not prepare myself more fully to receive Your holy gift, when the holy Patriarchs, Kings and Princes of old, with all their people, showed great devotion in Your holy worship?

The holy King David danced before the Ark with all his might,[10] recalling all the blessings to his ancestors. He made many musical instruments and devised psalms and taught his people to sing with joy. Filled with the Holy Spirit, he often sang and played the harp; he taught the people of Israel wholeheartedly to praise

God and to bless Him every day. If all these people performed such acts of worship and devotion before the Ark of the Covenant, how much greater devotion and reverence should I, and all Christian people, have in the presence of this Sacrament and in receiving the most wonderful Body of Christ.

Many people go on pilgrimages to different places to visit the relics of the Saints, amazed at the story of their lives and the splendour of their shrines.[11] They venerate and gaze at their bones, covered with silks and gold. But You are here on the altar, my God the Holy of Holies, Creator of humanity and Lord of the Angels. When people visit such places, they are often moved by curiosity and novelties and rarely do we hear that there is any amendment of life as a result, especially as their conversation is trivial and lacks real contrition. But here, in the Sacrament of the Altar, You are fully present, my God, the Man Jesus Christ. Here we freely partake of the fruit of eternal salvation, where we receive You reverently and devoutly. We are not attracted by levity, curiosity or sentimentality, but by firm faith, devout hope and sincere love.

O God, invisible Creator of the world, how wonderful are Your dealings with us! How sweetly and graciously You welcome the chosen to whom You give Yourself in this Sacrament! It passes all understanding. It kindles our love and draws the hearts of the faithful to Yourself. For in this most solemn Sacrament, Your faithful people, who strive to amend their whole lives, receive the grace of devotion and the love of virtue.

O the wonderful and hidden grace of this Sacrament! It is well known to Christ's faithful people, but it is hidden from unbelievers and servants of sin. In this Sacrament spiritual grace is conferred and lost virtue is restored to the soul, and sin-ravaged beauty is renewed. Such is the grace of this Sacrament that, through complete devotion, not only the mind but even the feeble body may receive greater strength.

We can only regret and deplore our negligence and lukewarmness, which prevents us from receiving Christ with greater love. For in Him lies all our virtue and hope of salvation. In Him is our holiness and liberation.[12] He is comfort to pilgrims, and the everlasting joy of the Saints. It is very sad that so many have little regard for this saving mystery, which delights heaven and sustains the whole world. Alas, we are so blind and our hearts so hard that we cannot fully appreciate this wonderful gift. By its frequent use, we can so easily respect it less.

If this most Holy Sacrament was only celebrated in one place and offered only by one priest in the whole world, we would all rush to that place and to that priest of God to share in the divine mysteries. But Christ is now offered in many places and there are many priests so that the grace and love of God may be widely known. Thus the Holy Communion is spread more extensively throughout the whole world.

We thank You, O good Jesus, eternal Shepherd, that You refresh us poor exiles with Your precious Body and Blood and invite us to receive these mysteries, saying, 'Come to Me, all you that are weary and are carrying heavy burdens, and I will give you rest.'

TWO

*On the great goodness and love of God revealed
to us in the Sacrament*

DISCIPLE: Lord, utterly trusting in Your goodness and great mercy, I come hungry to my Saviour, thirsty to the fountain of life[1] and needy to the King of Heaven, a creature to its Creator, desolate to my loving Consoler. Yet who am I that You should deign to come to me?[2] What am I that You should give Yourself to me? How dare a sinner stand before You in person? You know Your servant and see that there is nothing good to be worthy of this blessing. So I confess my lack of worth; I acknowledge Your excellence; I praise Your kindness and I offer my thankfulness for Your great love.[3] You do this of Your own will; not because of any virtues of mine, but solely that Your goodness will be very clear to me. Your love is more richly given to me, so that You may more perfectly commend humility to me. So, since it is Your desire and You have commanded it, I respect Your will; may it not be obstructed by any wickedness in me.

O most sweet and loving Jesus, You are owed deep reverence, thankfulness and everlasting praise when we receive Your sacred Body. No one on earth can properly explain its majesty. As I approach my Lord in Communion, what should my thoughts be? I cannot pay Him the honour that is due to Him, and yet I desire to receive Him devoutly. What better or more worthwhile desire can I have than to humble myself totally before You and to praise Your infinite goodness to me? So, my God, I praise You and will glorify You for ever, while, in the depths of my worthlessness, I despise and subordinate myself in Your presence.

Lord, You are the Holy of Holies; I am the worst of sinners. Yet, Lord, You bow before me, who am not worthy even to lift my eyes towards You, O Lord. You come to me and desire to be with me. You invite me to Your table.[4] You wish to feed me with the heavenly food, the bread of Angels.[5] This food is none other than You, the living Bread, which came down from heaven to give life to the world.[6]

See, from whom this love proceeds! See the source from which this glory shines! How deep a gratitude, how high praise are Your due for all these blessings! How greatly to our benefit and salvation was Your wisdom when You instituted this Sacrament! How sweet and delightful the feasts in which You give Yourself to be our food! How wonderful are Your ways, O Lord; how mighty Your power, how unerring Your truth! You spoke the Word, and all things were made.[7] You commanded and it was done.

It is wonderful, worthy of faith and transcending our minds, to consider how You, my Lord and God, true God and true man,[8] are completely present under the simple forms of bread and wine and are eaten without being destroyed by whoever receives You. O Lord of all, You stand in need of no one and yet, by means of this Sacrament, You are pleased to live in us.[9] Keep my heart and body untainted, so that with a glad and pure conscience I may be able to celebrate Your Holy Mysteries and to receive for my eternal salvation all those things that You have hallowed and instituted to Your own special honour and for Your perpetual memorial.

Be glad, my soul, and thank God for the noblest of all His gifts, for this special solace, bestowed on you in this vale of tears. For as often as you recall this mystery and receive the Body of Christ, you progress in the work of your redemption and share in the benefits of Christ. So commit yourself continually to the renewal of your mind,[10] and reflect deeply on the great mystery of redemption. When you celebrate or hear the Mass,[11] it should be as great, as new and joyful to you as if on the very day that Christ first came down into the Virgin's womb and was made man,[12] or, hanging on the Cross, suffered and died for our salvation.

THREE

On the value of frequent Communion[1]

DISCIPLE: My Lord, I come to You to receive the blessings of Your gift and to enjoy the feast that You have generously prepared for the poor. I find all that I can or should desire in You. You are my Saviour and my Redeemer, my hope and my strength,[2] my honour and my glory. So, Lord, gladden the soul of Your servant today, for to You I lift up my soul.[3] I desire to receive You with reverence and devotion. I long to invite You into my house so that, like Zacchaeus, I may gain Your blessing and be counted among Your chosen.[4] My soul longs to receive Your Body; my heart yearns to be united with You.[5]

It is enough if You give Yourself to me. Only You can provide satisfaction. I cannot exist without You. I cannot live unless You come to me. Therefore, I must approach You frequently and receive You as the remedy for salvation. For, if I am deprived of this heavenly food, I may faint on the way. For, O most merciful Jesus, it was You who, when You had been preaching to the crowds and healing their many diseases, said, 'I do not want to send them away hungry, for they might faint on the way.'[6] So now treat me in the same way. It was for the comfort of the faithful that You remained in this Sacrament. You are the sweet refreshment of the soul. Whoever receives You worthily will be a partaker and inheritor of eternal glory. I am so prone to frequent lapses and very quickly grow lukewarm and careless, that it is essential that I renew, cleanse and activate myself by frequent prayer and confession, and by the reception of Your Body. If I neglect it for any length of time, I may well fall away from my holy intention.

From youth onwards our senses are prone to evil.[7] Without

the help of this divine medicine[8] we soon lapse into greater wickedness. Holy Communion keeps us from evil and builds up goodness in us. For, if I am frequently careless and casual when I celebrate or communicate, what would happen to me if I were to neglect this remedy or fail to seek this most powerful assistance? And although I am neither fit nor in a proper state of mind to celebrate daily, yet I will try at proper times to receive Your Holy Mysteries and to present myself to receive this great gift. For as long as the faithful soul lives far from You in a mortal body, it is the greatest comfort that she can remember her God devoutly, and frequently receive her Beloved.

O Lord God, Creator and giver of life to all souls, Your kindness and mercy to us is wonderful. You stoop to visit the poor and humble soul and satisfy her hunger[9] with Your whole divinity and humanity. The soul that deserves to receive You with devotion is happy in mind, blessed in spirit and, in receiving You, is filled with spiritual joy! How great a Lord the soul receives! How beloved the Guest she welcomes! How delightful the Company she invites to enter! How faithful the Friend she makes! How gracious and noble the Spouse she embraces – one who is to be loved and desired above all others!

O dear and most beloved Lord, let heaven and earth, in all their beauty, keep silence before You.[10] Whatever praise and beauty they possess comes from Your generous goodness. They cannot approach the beauty of Your name and Your wisdom is infinite.[11]

FOUR

*On the many blessings granted to the
devout communicant*

DISCIPLE: My Lord God, lead Your servant with the blessings of Your goodness[1] so that I may approach Your glorious Sacrament devoutly and worthily. Stir up my heart to seek You and wake me from sleep. Visit me with Your salvation[2] so that my spirit may taste Your sweetness,[3] which is rightly concealed within this Sacrament like a fountain. Give light to my eyes to contemplate this great mystery. Give me strength to believe with unwavering faith. This is Your work and is not within the power of humans. It is through Your sacred institution and not a human invention. None of us are capable of grasping and understanding these things. They are beyond even the great knowledge of the Angels. How can I, an unworthy sinner (just dust and ashes), receive and understand so deep and sacred a mystery?

Lord, I approach You at Your command, in simplicity of heart,[4] in firm good faith and with hope and reverence. I firmly believe that You (both God and Man) are truly present in this Sacrament. It is Your desire that I should receive and be united to You in Your love. So I entreat You and beg You to give me special grace that I may fully melt and overflow in love for You and, thereafter, I may seek no comfort except in You. For this Most High and respected Sacrament is the medicine for all spiritual illness and health for soul and body. Through it our vices are cured, our passions restrained, our temptations are reduced, grace is given more totally and virtue, once established, is encouraged; faith is strengthened, hope is reinforced and love is inflamed and enlarged.

O my God, You have given, and still give, many blessings in this Sacrament to Your servants who make a devout Communion.

You are the guardian of my soul, the restorer of our weaknesses, and the giver of inner peace. The great comfort You give to us in our troubles lifts us up from the depths of despair to the hope of Your support. You restore and enlighten us with new blessings so that those who before they received Communion were desperate and lacking piety, find themselves renewed after the refreshment of this heavenly food and drink. You deliberately do this for Your loved ones so that they may truly know and endure their own weakness, and what blessings of grace they receive from You. For, in ourselves, we are cold, dry and indifferent, but through You we become eager, fervent and faithful. Will not all those who approach the fountain of sweetness with humility take away some of its sweetness with them? Or will not those who stand by a great fire benefit from some of its heat? You, Lord, are the always full and overflowing fountain. You are the ever-burning fire that can never be extinguished.

So, if I cannot draw from the fullness of the fountain[5] nor fully quench my thirst, I will still put my mouth to this heavenly spring and accept some drops to satisfy my thirst. Even if I may not become fully divine or fervent like the Cherubim and Seraphim,[6] I will still give myself to prayer and prepare my heart so that I may at least gain a portion of the holy fire by humbly receiving this life-giving Sacrament. O good Jesus, most holy Saviour, I ask You in Your mercy and grace to give me what is lacking in me. For You graciously call us to Yourself saying, 'Come to Me, all you that are weary and are carrying heavy burdens, and I will give you rest.'

I labour in the sweat of my brow.[7] I am tortured by grief of heart. I am burdened by my sins.[8] I am troubled by temptations and trapped by many evil passions. No one can help; no one can liberate and save, except You, O Lord God, my Saviour. So I commit myself, and all that I have, to You, so that You may guard and guide me to eternal life. Accept me for the praise and glory of Your name, for You have given Your Body and Blood to be my food and drink. O Lord God, my Saviour, through the reception of Your Mysteries, grant me an increase in committed devotion.

FIVE

On the value of the Sacrament and the priestly office

CHRIST: If you had the purity of the Angels and the holiness of St John the Baptist you would still be unworthy to receive or touch this Sacrament. For it is not because of any personal merit that someone is allowed to consecrate or handle the Sacrament of Christ and to receive the bread of Angels.[1] The office of a priest is high and of great dignity, for the priest is granted what is not even offered to Angels. For only a properly ordained priest of the Church has the power to celebrate and consecrate the Body of Christ. The priest is the minister of God, and uses the words of God at His own command and appointment; but God Himself is the chief agent and the invisible operator to whose will all things are subject[2] and whose commands all creatures obey.

In all that relates to this most excellent Sacrament, you should have regard to God's Word, rather than your own perceptions or any visible sign. So when you approach the altar do so with awe and reverence. Consider from whom this ministry proceeds. It has been delivered to you through the imposition of hands by the bishop.[3] You have been made a priest and ordained to celebrate the Sacrament. So ensure that you offer this sacrifice to God faithfully, regularly and devoutly with a life that is above reproach.[4] Your obligations are now greater, you exercise tighter bonds of discipline and need to aim for a higher degree of holiness. A priest should be adorned with all virtues and demonstrate a holy life to others.[5] A priest's life should not be like that of worldly people but like that of the Angels,[6] or those without fault on earth.

A priest robed in sacred vestments takes the place of Christ in order humbly to intercede with God for priests and for all people.[7] The priest wears the sign of the Cross, both in front and behind, in order to be perpetually reminded of our Lord's Passion. In front the chasuble[8] bears the Cross, so that the priest may carefully follow in Christ's footsteps and ardently follow them.[9] The priest's shoulders are marked with the Cross in order, in mercy and love, to carry every personal injury done by others. The priest wears the Cross in front to express penitence for sins, and behind in order to be compassionate and lament the sins of others. Remembering always that the priest is appointed as a mediator between God and the sinner, the priest will never cease from prayer and the holy sacrifice to try and deserve grace and mercy. By celebrating [this Sacrament], the priest honours God and gives joy to the Angels. The priest builds up the Church, helps the living, gains rest for the departed and so participates in all good things.

SIX

How should we prepare for Communion?

DISCIPLE: When I consider Your majesty and my own wretch-edness, I am full of fear and confusion. For if I do not accept You, I refuse life; and if I participate unworthily I will incur Your displeasure. What then shall I do, my God, my helper, my counsellor in need? Show me the right way[1] and provide me with some short devotion suitable for Holy Communion. I need to prepare my heart for You, devoutly and reverently, both for the receiving of Your Sacrament and for the proper offering of such a great and holy sacrifice.

SEVEN

By self-examination and resolving to do better

CHRIST: It is important above all else that, when celebrating, a priest has humility of heart and deep reverence when handling or receiving the Sacrament and does so with firmness of faith and with the real intention of giving glory to God. So examine your conscience carefully. You can, by true contrition and humble confession, to the best of your ability cleanse and purify it. So you will not hold back any grave matter that may prevent you from approaching the Sacrament. Disapprove of all your general sins and your troubling sins in particular. And, if time allows, confess to God the secrets of your heart and the misery of your passions.[1]

Grieve that you are so carnal and worldly
So undisciplined in your enthusiasms
So full of bodily lusts
So unguarded in your outward perceptions
So often engrossed in trivial fantasies
So absorbed in mundane matters
So unconcerned about spiritual matters
So easily moved to laughter and frivolity
So negligent of sorrow and penitence
So keen for comfort and self-indulgence
So averse to commitment and self-discipline
So anxious for news and sight-seeing
So reluctant to appreciate humble and simple things
So greedy for many possessions
So reluctant to give generously
So persistent in possessing

So unguarded in speaking
So reluctant to remain silent
So disruptive in manners
So impetuous in action
So greedy for food
So deaf to the Word of God
So quick to rest
So slow to work
So alert to gossip
So drowsy at holy vigils
So hurried in your prayers
So rambling in concentration
So careless at keeping the hours of prayer[2]
So apathetic at the Eucharist
So lacking in devotion at Communion
So easily distracted
So rarely fully attentive
So suddenly stirred to anger
So quick to take offence
So ready to judge others
So severe in reprimanding
So cheerful when all is well
So weak when things go wrong
So often promising good deeds, and so rarely doing them.

Thus, when you have confessed and regretted all these and other faults, with deep sorrow, penitence at your weakness, make a strong resolution to amend your life and go forward into holiness. Surrender yourself and your will entirely to Me and offer yourself on the altar of your heart, as a perpetual sacrifice to the honour of My name. In faith commit yourself, body and soul, to Me, so that you may worthily approach and offer the sacrifice to God, and receive the Sacrament of My Body for your soul's health.

There is no better offering, or greater satisfaction for the washing away of sins, than to offer ourselves totally and purely to God, together with the offering of the Body of Christ at the Mass and in Communion.[3] When someone is truly penitent and makes an effort to come to Me for pardon and grace, I will put away all sins and forgive them all.[4] 'I live,' says the Lord, 'I have no pleasure in the death of the wicked, but that the wicked turn from their ways and live.'[5]

EIGHT

Christ's offering on the Cross

CHRIST: I hung naked on the Cross with My arms outstretched, giving Myself freely to God the Father for your sins.[1] My whole being was a sacrifice of holy propitiation.[2] In the same way you must willingly offer yourself daily to Me in the Eucharist with all your power and tenderness as a pure and holy offering. I require nothing less of you than that you should surrender yourself totally to Me.[3] I regard as nothing anything you offer apart from yourself. I do not seek a token gift, but yourself.[4]

If you owned everything in the world, apart from Me nothing would satisfy you; so nothing you give to Me is acceptable, apart from yourself. Offer yourself to Me and give yourself totally to God and this will make your sacrifice acceptable.[5] I gave Myself totally to the Father for you. I have given My actual Body and Blood to be your food, so that I may be all yours and that you may be Mine for ever. But if you put your trust in yourself and do not give yourself freely to My will, your offering is incomplete; nor can our union be perfect. If you wish to find freedom and grace, the free gift of yourself into the hands of God must precede everything else. The reason why so few gained inward illumination and freedom is because they were unable completely to deny themselves. My words are unalterable: 'If you are not prepared to leave all your possessions behind you cannot be my disciples.'[6] So if you wish to be My disciple, offer yourself to Me with all your heart.

NINE

We should offer ourselves totally to God and pray for everyone

DISCIPLE: Lord, everything in heaven and on earth is Yours.[1] I wish to give myself to You as a free offering and to belong to You for ever. With simplicity of heart, O Lord, I offer myself to You today to be Your servant for ever.[2] I do this as an act of obedience and as an act of perpetual praise. Accept me, together with the holy offering of Your precious Body, which I plead before You this day in the unseen presence of adoring Angels, for my salvation and that of all Your people.

Lord, I offer on Your altar of reconciliation all the sins and offences which I have ever committed before You and Your Holy Angels, from the first day of my sin until now. Burn and consume them all in the fire of Your love. Blot out the stains of my sins[3] and give me a clean conscience.[4] Restore the grace lost by my sin. Grant me total forgiveness of all offences, and of Your mercy receive me with a kiss of peace.[5]

What can I do to have my sins taken away but to humbly confess them and incessantly call on Your forgiveness? Hear me, O my God, I beg, in Your mercy, as I stand before You. All my sins are utterly hateful to me, and I resolve never to commit them again. I repent of them and will grieve for them as long as I live. I am ready to do penance[6] and to make any amends that I can. Forgive me, O God, forgive me for Your holy name's sake[7] and save this soul whom You have redeemed through Your precious Blood.[8] I commit myself totally to Your mercy, and place myself completely in Your hands. Treat me according to Your goodness, and not as my wickedness deserves.[9]

Also, I offer to You whatever is good in me, even if it is small and imperfect, so that You may strengthen and bless my being to make it precious and acceptable to You and to raise it continually towards perfection. So, Lord, bring me, lazy and useless as I am, to a worthy and blessed end.

I offer You also all the desires of devout people, the needs of my parents, friends, brothers, sisters and all who are close to me, and the needs of all who have desired and asked me to pray and offer the Mass for them. I pray that they may all, both living and departed, enjoy the help of Your grace, the aid of Your comfort, protection from dangers and deliverance from the suffering to come. So that, freed from all evils, they may offer great praise and thanks to You.

Also, I offer You my prayers especially for those who have, in any way, injured, grieved or reviled me, or who have done me harm or pain. Similarly for any whom I have hurt, troubled, injured or offended by word or action, consciously or unconsciously. So that You may in mercy forgive all our sins and offences against one another. O Lord, remove from our hearts all suspicion, ill feeling, anger and contention and whatever may upset love or mutual affection. Have mercy, O Lord, have mercy on all who ask for Your forgiveness.[10] Give grace to those who badly need it; and help us all to live that we may profitably enjoy Your love, and finally come to everlasting life.

TEN

That Holy Communion should not be lightly abandoned

CHRIST: Come frequently to the fountain of grace and divine mercy, the fountain of goodness and total purity, so that you may be healed from all your passions and vices and be made more vigilant and strong to resist all the temptations and deceits of the Devil. For the Enemy knows very well the abundant fruit and the great remedies that are provided in Holy Communion. He tries every means in his power to impede and prevent the faithful and devout people from receiving it.

Satan's most violent assaults come upon some people when they prepare for Holy Communion. As it is written in the Book of Job,[1] the evil spirit comes among the children of God to disturb them with his accustomed malice, or to make them frightened and perplexed. In this way he seeks to reduce their love for God or to destroy their faith, so that, if possible, they may completely abandon Communion, or come to it with little fervour. But pay no attention to his traps and cunning illusions, however vile and horrible. Throw back these fantasies onto his own head. Treat him with the contempt and mockery he deserves. Never abandon Holy Communion because of his insults and distractions.

Some people are held back by their sense of piety, or anxieties about confession. When this happens seek the advice of a wise teacher, and put aside all misgivings, for this is an obstacle to devotion. Do not delay in receiving Communion because of small doubts or anxieties, but go at once to confession and willingly forgive those who have offended you. If you have offended anyone, humbly ask pardon and God will readily forgive you.

What use is it to put off confession or receiving Communion? Purify yourself at once. Spew out the poison quickly, and receive the medicine without delay. Swift action will help more than procrastination. If you delay, for any reason, today, something worse may happen to you tomorrow. So you will be kept from Communion for a long time and become even more unfit. Shake off your sloth and dullness as quickly as possible. It is no advantage to remain upset and in distress for a long time, nor to stay away from the sacred mysteries because of mundane problems. Far from it; it is hurtful to delay Communion over a long period, for this often leads to sloth and spiritual dryness.

Sadly, some half-hearted and careless people grab any excuse to postpone their confession and desire, for that reason, to put off Holy Communion because they are unwilling to be committed to a more vigilant life. Those who so lightly put off Holy Communion are lacking in love and are weak in devotion. Happy and dear to God are those who keep their hearts and their lives pure. They are eager and well prepared to communicate every day, if it were possible, and might do so without seeming to be unusual. However, those who sometimes abstain out of humility, or are genuinely prevented, can be commended for their reverence. But if sloth takes over, we must resist it with all our energy, and God will strengthen our desire by reason of our good intentions, which God specially favours.

When someone is unavoidably absent, then as long as the desire and the good will for Communion remains, there is no loss of the fruits of the Sacrament. For anyone who sincerely desires it can, on any day or at any time, make unhindered an act of spiritual Communion[2] with Christ for the soul's benefit. However, special feasts and certain seasons should be observed for receiving the Body of our Saviour sacramentally with love and reverence, to give honour and praise to God, more than for our own satisfaction. When anyone receives mystic communion and invisible food, they devoutly recall the mystery of the Incarnation and Passion of Christ, and are stirred to fresh love of Him. But those who only prepare before a festival, or when religious custom requires it, will often be unprepared.

Blessed are those who, whenever they celebrate or communicate, offer themselves as a living sacrifice. And, when celebrating, be neither too slow nor too hurried, but observe the common practice of those with whom you are living.[3] Try not to cause irritation or weariness to others, but to observe the customs appointed by the Fathers. Consider the needs of others before your own personal devotional preferences.

ELEVEN

*How the Body of Christ and the Holy Scriptures
are necessary for the faithful soul*

DISCIPLE: O sweet Lord Jesus, how great is the joy of the faithful soul who feasts at Your banquet, where the food set before us is none other than Your real self. This is most beloved, and all that the heart desires. How deeply I want to pour out my fervent tears in Your presence and, like the devout Magdalene, wash Your feet with my tears.[1] But where is my devotion? And where is this flood of holy tears?[2] Surely Your presence and that of Your Holy Angels should make my heart burn and cry for joy! For in Your Holy Sacrament, You are actually present with me, albeit concealed under a different form.

I could not bear to gaze on You in the total glory of Your divinity, nor could the whole world cope with the brightness and glory of Your majesty. So You tolerate my frailty and hide Yourself in this Holy Sacrament. Here I actually possess and adore Him to whom the Angels do homage in heaven.[3] I do so by faith alone, but they do it by unconcealed sight.[4] I must be content with the light of true faith, and stay like that until the day of endless glory comes and the shadows are dispersed.[5] When the wholeness comes,[6] the use of Sacraments will come to an end. The blessed in glory need no sacramental healing. They rejoice in the presence of God for ever, and view His unveiled glory.[7] Transformed from glory[8] into the glory of His own unsearchable divinity, they taste the Word of God made man, as He was[9] from the beginning and as He remains for ever.[10]

Aware of these wonders, even spiritual consolation seems tedious. For as long as I cannot see my Lord in His unseen glory, all that I can see or hear in this world I find worthless. My God, You are my witness[11] that nothing can comfort me, nor can I be content with any created thing except in You alone, my God, whom I desire to contemplate for eternity. But, in this mortal life, this is not possible for me, so I have to use great patience and surrender all my desires to You. During their lives, Your Holy Saints, who now share Your joy in the Kingdom of Heaven, waited for the coming of Your glory with patience and faith.[12] What they believed, I believe. What they hoped to enjoy, I hope to enjoy. Where they arrived by Your grace, I hope to arrive. Meanwhile I will walk by faith, encouraged by the example of the Saints.[13] The Holy Scriptures will be my comfort and my stimulation, and, above all else, Your sacred Body will be my special remedy and refuge.

I now realize that there are two things of the greatest importance to me, without which this miserable life would be unbearable. While imprisoned in this human body, I realize the need for two things – food and light. So, in my weakness, You have provided Your sacred Body to refresh my soul and body, and put Your Word as a lamp to my feet.[14] I cannot rightly live without these two. For the Word of God is the light to the soul and Your Sacrament is the bread of life.[15] You might call them the two tables set on either side of the treasure house of the Holy Church. One is the table of the holy altar, having on it the holy bread,[16] the precious Body of Christ. The other is the divine law containing holy doctrine, teaching true faith and the steadfast way, even into the veil that guards the Holy of Holies.[17]

O good Jesus, Light eternal, I thank You for the teaching concerning Your holy table, which You have given us through Your servants the Prophets, Apostles and other teachers.[18] I thank You, Creator and Redeemer of all, that You have revealed to the whole world the depths of Your love. You have prepared a great supper[19] at which You provide us, not with the Lamb of the old law, but Your most holy Body and Blood to be our food. You give joy to all the faithful, enabling them to drink deeply from the cup of salvation.[20] This contains all the joys of heaven, where the Angels share the feast with us, but with even greater sweetness.

How great and worthy is the office of a priest to whom is given the authority to consecrate, with the holy words of the

Lord of Majesty, to bless Him with their lips, to hold Him in their hands, to accept Him in their mouths and to minister Him to others!

How clean should be the hands, how pure the lips, how holy the body, how spotless the heart of the priest, to whom the author of all purity is entrusted! Nothing should come from the mouth of a priest, who so often receives the Sacrament of Christ, than what is holy, true and edifying. May the priest's eyes, which so often look on the Body of Christ, be simple and modest. May the priest's hands, which handle the Creator of heaven and earth, be pure and lifted up to heaven.[21] For the words of the law – 'You shall be holy, for I the Lord your God am holy'[22] – are addressed especially to priests.

Almighty God, may Your grace assist us so that we, who have undertaken the office of priesthood, are enabled to serve You worthily and devoutly, with integrity and a good conscience. While it is not possible to remain in complete innocence of life, as we ought, grant us to repent of our sins honestly, and thereafter to serve You with deeper devotion in the spirit of humility and determined goodwill.

TWELVE

On the great care needed to receive Christ in Communion

CHRIST: I am the lover of purity and the giver of all holiness. I look for a pure heart to be My resting place.[1] Prepare and make ready for Me a large upper room, and there I will eat the Passover with you.[2] If you want Me to come and live with you, dispose of the old leaven,[3] and clean out the habitation of your heart.[4] Shut out the whole world and its vicious uproar; and stay there alone, like a solitary sparrow on a rooftop.[5] Acknowledge the digressions of your soul[6] in bitterness. Every loving person reveals their affection by preparing the best and finest room for a close friend.

But you know that even your best preparations cannot be worthy of Me, even if you were to prepare for a whole year and do absolutely nothing else. Only by My mercy and grace are you permitted to approach My table. It is like a beggar who, being invited to a rich person's table, is unable to offer anything in return except humble gratitude.[7] Do whatever you can and do it diligently, not out of habit or necessity, but with awe and reverent love to receive the Body of your Lord and God, who kindly comes to you. It is My invitation and My command. I will supply whatever is lacking in you. So come and receive Me.[8]

When I grant you the grace of devotion, offer thanks to God, not because you deserve to enjoy it, but because I have had mercy on you. If you feel no devotion and suffer from a dry soul, persevere in prayer. Groan, knock[9] and persist until you may be worthy to receive some crumb or drop of saving grace. You have need of Me; I have no need of you.[10] You do not come to sanctify Me, but I come to sanctify you and lift you up. You come to be blessed and united to Me, so that you may receive new grace from God and be inspired afresh to amend your life. Do not neglect this grace.[11] Always prepare yourself with great care, and invite the Beloved into your heart.

Not only must you prepare devoutly before Communion, but also continue your prayer after receiving the Sacrament. As much care is needed after Communion as the devout preparation before it. Great watchfulness is the best preparation for receiving richer graces. Those who return to outward pleasures will not be willing to do this. Beware of a lot of talk.[12] Stay in a quiet place and enjoy the presence of God; for you hold Him, whom the whole world cannot remove from you. I am He to whom you need to offer your whole being so that, free from care, you may no longer live in yourself but in Me.[13]

THIRTEEN

*How the heart and soul should seek union
with Christ in His Sacrament*

DISCIPLE: Lord, if only I might seek You alone, so that I can open my heart to You and rejoice in You, as my soul desires. Then no one would ever despise me, nor any creature disturb or notice me, so that You alone might speak to me and I to You, as lovers speak to each other, face to face, or like a conversation between friends.[1] It is my prayer and desire to be totally united to You and to remove my heart from all created things and increasingly delight in heavenly and eternal things, through Holy Communion and frequent celebration of the Mass. O my Lord and God,[2] when shall I be wholly united to and absorbed into You and unaware of my self? You in me and I in You, may we abide in one for ever.[3]

You are indeed my Beloved, a paragon among ten thousand,[4] in whom my soul rejoices to dwell all the days of my life.[5] You are indeed the giver of peace, in whom is perfect peace and true rest, without which there is nothing but labour, sadness and endless misery. You are indeed the one true and hidden God,[6] whose dealings are not with the wicked but with the simple and humble.[7] Lord, how sweet it is for Your Spirit to reveal Your graciousness to Your children, refreshing them with the most sweet bread, which comes down from heaven.[8] 'No nation, however great, has a god so close at hand, but the Lord our God is close to us.'[9] You comfort the faithful daily and raise their hearts to heaven by giving Yourself to be their food and delight.

What other race is so favoured as Christian people? What creature under heaven is so blessed as the devout soul into whom God enters, thus sustaining them with His glorious Body? O unutterable grace, O admirable worthiness, O boundless love dispensed only to humanity. 'What shall I return to the Lord for all His bounty to me?'[10] Nothing that I can give will be more acceptable to Him than my whole heart becoming inwardly united to Him in total surrender. When my soul is fully united to God, my whole being will be filled with joy. Then He will say to Me, 'If you abide in Me, I will abide in you',[11] and I shall answer Him, 'Lord, live with me I pray, for I will gladly stay with You. My only desire is that my heart be united to You.'

FOURTEEN

On the zealous desire for the Body of Christ

DISCIPLE: Lord, what treasures of loving kindness do You preserve for those who fear You.[1] When I reflect on those devout Christians who attend Your Sacrament with the deepest devotion and love, I feel ashamed and astonished that I approach Your altar and the table for Holy Communion with such a cold and lukewarm heart. I remain so miserly and lacking in love. So my heart does not burn within me in Your presence and I am neither strongly drawn, nor lovingly disposed, as many devout people have been. For, out of their zealous desire for Communion and deep love for You, they cannot hold back their tears but out of the depth of their souls yearn, both with the heart and body, for You, O God, the source of living water.[2] There was no other way in which they could gratify or satisfy their hunger except by receiving Your Body, with great joy and eagerness of spirit.

How true was their enthusiastic faith, which was in itself a clear expression of Your divine presence. For they really know their Lord in the breaking of bread, whose hearts burn within them so fully when Jesus walks with them.[3] I rarely feel such devout affection and unconditional love. O good and kind Jesus have mercy on me and grant to me, Your miserable beggar, to feel at least sometimes a bit of that deepest desire for Your love in Holy Communion. Thus my faith may be strengthened; my hope in Your goodness may be encouraged; and love, once fully ignited, having tasted the bread of heaven, may never die out. Your generosity is strong enough to give me even this grace which I desire. So grant me, I pray, when it shall please You of Your grace and kindness, the spirit of enthusiasm. For, though I do not burn with such zealous desire as those who are totally devoted to You, I long to have that great and burning desire. I plead and pray that, through Your grace, I may have a part with all Your true lovers and be numbered in their holy company.

FIFTEEN

*How true devotion is gained through
humility and self-denial*

CHRIST: You must seek the grace of holiness with commitment. Ask for it with real desire, wait for it with patience and trust, receive it with gratitude, sustain it with humility, use it carefully, and leave to God the time and nature of His heavenly gift. Above all, when you feel little or no inner passion, humble yourself, and do not be too depressed or discouraged. God will often grant you, in a brief moment, what He has withheld for a long time. Also sometimes He grants at the right moment what He delayed to give when you first asked.

If grace were always granted immediately and were available for the asking, our weakness could barely sustain it. Therefore the grace of holiness must be anticipated with firm hope and humble patience. When it is not granted or is withdrawn, realize that this is due to you and your own sinfulness. Grace may be hindered or concealed by some very trivial matter (if anything can be called trivial, and not serious, which obstructs such a great good). But when you have removed the obstacle, whether small or great, and have fully overcome it, then you will have your desire.

As soon as you surrender yourself to God with all your being and seek nothing for your own will and pleasure, but put yourself totally at His disposal, you will find yourself united to Him and at peace. Nothing will offer you more joy and satisfaction than accomplishing God's will. So those who would aspire to seek God with a pure heart[1] and who disengage themselves from all excessive love or hatred of any created thing, will be best fitted to receive grace and be worthy of the gifts of sanctity. For our Lord gives His blessings where He finds empty vessels ready to receive them.[2] The more fully we renounce worldly things and the more fully we die to ourselves by self-renunciation, the quicker grace will be given, the more richly it will permeate, and the closer to God it will lift up the heart which will be free from the world.

Such people will be enriched with joy and wonder, and their hearts will be radiant with gladness.[3] For the hand of the Lord is upon them, and they have entrusted themselves into His hands for ever. So a person will be blessed who seeks God wholeheartedly.[4] They will not have received their soul in vain. When they receive the Holy Eucharist they earn that grace which is union with God. For they do not think about their own devotion and solace, but beyond all such devotion and solace they seek the honour and glory of God.

SIXTEEN

How we should declare our needs to
Christ and ask for His grace

DISCIPLE: Most dear and loving Lord, by whom I now desire to be accepted in total devotion, You know my weakness and my great needs, the many sins and vices that afflict me, and how I am often discouraged, tempted, troubled and corrupted. I come to You for healing. I plead with You to strengthen and relieve me. I pray to Him who knows all things,[1] to whom even my deepest thoughts are revealed, and who alone can fully support and help me. You know the good things I need above all else, and my great lack of virtue.

Look on me, Lord, as I stand before You, naked and poor, begging for grace and pleading for mercy. Satisfy the hunger of this, Your beggar. Warm my coldness with the fire of Your love and remove my blindness through the light of Your presence.[2] Make all worldly things unattractive to me; make me patient of all damaging and harmful things. Help me to be contemptuous of and remove from my mind all created things and all below You. Lift my heart up to You in heaven and let me no longer be a vagrant on earth.[3] From now on, may my only joy be to be with You, now and for ever, my food and drink, my love and my joy, my delight and my total good.

O that Your presence would set me totally on fire, and transform me into Yourself, so that, through the grace of inner union and by dissolving into passionate love, I might be made one in spirit with You.[4] Do not send me away hungry and thirsty, but treat me with Your mercy, as You have treated Your Saints so generously. How wonderful it would be if You inflamed me, dead to myself; for You, Lord, are the everlasting fire which burns for ever.[5] You are the love which purifies the heart[6] and illuminates the mind.

SEVENTEEN

*On the burning love and eager
desire to adore Christ*

DISCIPLE: Dear Lord, I long to receive You with all my devotion and burning love, and with all the affection and zeal of my heart, just as many Saints and holy people have longed to receive You in Communion. They were especially pleasing to You by the holiness of their lives and were on fire with devotion. O my God, eternal love, my greatest good and everlasting delight, I desire to receive You with the most ardent devotion and greatest reverence that any of Your Saints have ever felt, or could feel.

Unlike them, I am not fit to enjoy such feelings of devotion. Yet I offer You all the love in my heart, as if I alone were moved by these appropriate and burning desires. So I offer You whatever a devout heart can conceive or desire with all reverence and love. I wish to hold back no part of myself and freely and most gladly to surrender to You all that I am or have. O Lord my God, my Creator and Redeemer, I want to accept You today with all that affection, reverence, praise and honour, with that gratitude, nobility and love, with that faith, hope and purity with which Your most holy Mother, the glorious Virgin Mary, desired and received You when she devoutly and humbly answered the Angel who brought the joyful message of the mystery of the Incarnation: 'Here am I, the servant of the Lord; let it be with me according to your word.'[1]

And as did Your most holy forerunner, John the Baptist (that most excellent of Saints), who was glad and leapt for joy,[2] praising the Holy Spirit, while still in his mother's womb, and who when he later saw Jesus walking among the people[3] devoutly and lovingly humbled himself, saying: 'The friend of

the bridegroom, who stands and hears him, rejoices greatly at
the bridegroom's voice.'[4] Just like him, I wish to be aflame with
great and holy desires and to surrender myself to You with all
my heart. So I offer and lay before You the praises, the worship, which You receive from all zealous hearts – their outbursts
of happy praise, their ardent affection, their ecstatic experiences, their spiritual insights and their heavenly visions. I add
to these all the goodness and praises that ever have been or will
be offered to You in heaven or on earth. I plead them for myself
and for all who have been commended to my prayers, so that
You may be worthily praised and magnified for ever.[5]

Receive, O Lord my God, my vows, my desire to give You
everlasting praise and endless blessing. They are properly due
to You because of Your immeasurable greatness.[6] I surrender
all, and wish to do so every day and at every moment of time.
I lovingly pray and plead with the entire heavenly host to join
with all the faithful in giving You praise and thanksgiving.

May all races and tribes, nations and languages[7] praise and
magnify Your sweet and holy name with joy and zealous devotion. May all who reverently and devoutly celebrate Your
wonderful Sacrament and receive it with total faith to gain
Your grace and mercy, humbly intercede for me, a sinner. So
when they who have won the devotion (which they desired)
and the blessed union with Yourself (which will bring them joy)
and, greatly consoled and refreshed, have left Your sacred and
heavenly table, You may, in generosity, remember me and my
poverty.

EIGHTEEN

*How we should not curiously examine the
Holy Sacrament but humbly imitate Christ,
submitting our reason to the holy faith*

CHRIST: Beware of curious and vain attempts to analyse the Sacrament, which goes much deeper than the human mind can grasp, for 'The quest for glory is onerous.'[1] The actions of God are greater than we can understand. But we may lovingly and humbly seek for the truth as long as we are willing to learn from others, and try to walk in the paths of the wisdom and teachings of the Fathers.[2]

They are happy who can simply turn away from difficult questions and go ahead on the clear and open path of God's commandments.[3] Many people lose their sense of devotion by trying to understand the mysteries of God, which are beyond them. It is faith God requires of you and a holy life, not great understanding of deep mysteries. If you cannot understand things that are beneath you, how can you grasp these things, which are above you? Submit yourself to God, humbly submit yourself to the faith and you will be given in the light of knowledge all you find necessary and useful.

Many people have great temptations about the faith and the Sacrament. They should blame their enemy the Devil, not themselves. Do not be anxious; do not resist your thoughts, or attempt to answer any doubts which the Devil suggests. Trust in God's Word; believe in His Saints and Prophets and the evil enemy will run away from you.[4] It can be very beneficial for the servants of God to experience such doubts, as the Devil does not tempt unbelievers and sinners who already belong to him, but he tempts and tests the faithful and devout in every way he can.

Go forward then with simple, undoubting faith, and come to the Sacrament with humble reverence, confidently committing to Almighty God whatever you are not able to understand. God never deceives us, but we are deceived when we put too much trust in ourselves.

God walks with the simple,[5]
shows Himself to the humble,
gives understanding to the innocent,
reveals His secrets to the pure
and conceals His grace from the proud and curious.[6]

All reason and natural enquiry must follow from faith, not precede or encroach upon it.[7] For in this sublime and Holy Sacrament, faith and love take priority over everything else. It works in ways we do not understand. The eternal God, transcendent and infinite in power, does great and unsearchable things,[8] both in heaven and on earth,[9] and His understanding cannot be fathomed.[10] For, if the works of God could be easily understood, they would be neither inscrutable nor unutterable.

PART FOUR

THE CHAPTERS OF
BOOK THREE

Here begins the Book of
Inner Consolation

ONE

How Christ speaks inwardly to the soul

'Let me hear what God the Lord will speak.'[1]

Blessed are the souls to whom the Lord speaks[2] and accept the comfort of His Word. Blessed are your ears that hear[3] the divine faint murmuring sound[4] and disregard the whispers of the world. Blessed are the ears that listen clearly to the inward teaching of the truth rather than the muttering voices of the world. Blessed are the eyes that are shut to external things but are fixed on inwards things. Blessed are those who penetrate into inner things and prepare every day to accept the secrets of heaven. Blessed are those who strive to be totally devoted to God and who free themselves from all the snares of the world.

O my soul, reflect on these things, and firmly shut the door against sensual desires so that you may hear what your Lord God is saying within you. For the Beloved says, 'I am your salvation,[5] your peace and your life; keep close to Me and you will find peace.' Dismiss the transitory and grasp at the eternal. For what are the things of time but deceptions? How can any creature help you if your Creator deserts you? So put aside all else and make yourself acceptable to your Creator and be faithful to Him, so that you may take hold of real sanctification.

TWO

How truth speaks inwardly through silence

DISCIPLE: 'Speak, Lord, for Your servant is listening.'[1] 'I am Your servant; give me understanding, so that I may know Your decrees.'[2] 'Turn my heart to Your decrees.'[3] Let Your speech descend on me like the dew.[4] The people of Israel said to Moses, 'You speak to us, and we will listen; but do not let God speak to us, or we will die.'[5] I do not pray like this, O Lord, but with the Prophet Samuel I humbly and earnestly beg, 'Speak, Lord, for Your servant is listening.' Do not let Moses or the Prophets speak to me, but may You speak to me, O Lord God, for it is You who inspired and enlightened the Prophets. Without You they could do nothing. Only You can really instruct me without their help.

The Prophets can preach the Word, but they are unable to confer the Spirit. They utter fine words, but if You are silent, they cannot inspire the heart. They give us the writing, but You reveal the meaning. They expose the mysteries, but You expose the meaning of the secrets. They teach Your laws, but You give us the strength to follow them. They point the way, but You grant us the strength to follow it. Their action is external, but You instruct and enlighten the heart. They water the seed, but You make it grow.[6] They preach the Word, but You give understanding to the mind.

So do not let Moses speak to me, but You, O Lord my God, the everlasting Truth, in case I die and bear no fruit. I am warned only by words but not enthused in my heart for fear it results in my condemnation if I hear Your Word but do not obey it, know Your Word but do not love it, believe it but do not keep it. So speak, Lord, Your servant is listening. 'You have the words of eternal life.'[7] Speak to me, Lord, and comfort my soul. Turn my life to Your praise, glory and everlasting honour.

THREE

On hearing the Word of God with humility

CHRIST: My child, hear My words. They are of great sweetness and exceed the learning of the philosophers and the wise of this world. My words are both Spirit and life[1] and beyond your understanding. They are not to be quoted out of vain pleasure, but are to be heard quietly[2] and accepted in humility and love.

DISCIPLE: 'Happy are those whom You discipline, O Lord, and whom You teach out of Your law.'[3] You restore them from misfortune and so they will not be desolate on the earth.

CHRIST: I have taught the Prophets from the beginning of the world.[4] I do not cease to speak to people today; but many are hardened and deaf to My voice. Many pay more attention to the world than to God, and prefer to follow their bodily desires rather than becoming acceptable to God. The world is served with great enthusiasm and promises transitory rewards of no value. I promise everlasting and rich rewards, but people's hearts are hardened to them. Who is there who serves and obeys Me with as much enthusiasm as they serve the world and its rulers? 'Be ashamed, O Sidon, for the sea has spoken.'[5] If you ask why this is, I will give you the reason.

For a very little reward, someone will rush away on a long journey, while many would hardly take a single step to gain eternal life. People look for trifling gains; they will quarrel shamefully over a single coin; they will work all day and night for nothing but a vague promise. What a shame! They are unwilling to suffer a little toil to gain an imperishable good, a reward beyond price, and the highest honour and unending glory. O reluctant and complaining servant! It is your shame that worldly people are more prepared for damnation than you are for salvation. They are more willing to seek vanity than you are willing to pursue the truth. Often, they are deceived in their aspirations but no one is ever deceived by My promises. Never did I send anyone who trusts in Me away empty. I give what I promise; I will perform what I have proclaimed, as long as you remain faithful to the end. I will reward all good people and vindicate all the faithful.

It will help you at times of temptation to write My words in your heart[6] and consider them deeply. When you are reading, whatever you do not understand, you will discover on the day of My coming. I visit My chosen ones in two ways: with testing and with consolation. Each day I teach them two lessons. One when I correct their faults, the other when I encourage them to progress in virtue. 'The one who rejects Me and does not receive My Word has a judge; on the last day the Word that I have spoken will serve as judge.'[7]

A PRAYER FOR THE GRACE
OF DEVOTION

DISCIPLE: O Lord my God, You are my total good. Who am I that I should dare to speak to You?[8] I am the poorest of Your servants and a miserable worm, much poorer and more worthless than I can ever understand or explain. Yet, Lord, remember that I am nothing. I have nothing, I can do nothing.[9] You alone are just, good and holy. You can do all things, give all things, fill all things[10] and leave only the wicked with nothing. 'Be mindful of Your mercy, O Lord, and of Your steadfast love,'[11] and fill my heart with Your grace. For it is Your will that none of Your deeds should be empty. Can I endure my life of sorrows, unless You strengthen me with Your grace and mercy? Do not hide Your face from me.[12] Do not delay Your coming. Do not remove Your consolation from me in case my soul becomes like a dry desert.[13] Teach me to do Your will,[14] teach me to live well and humbly in Your sight. You are my wisdom. You know me well and knew me before the world was made and before I existed.[15]

FOUR

On living in truth and humility
in the sight of God

CHRIST: My child, walk before Me in truth, and continually seek Me with a blameless heart.[1] Those who walk with Me in truth will be protected against the attacks of evil and freed from deceivers and the slanders of the wicked. If truth sets you free[2] you are free indeed, and you can ignore the vain words of others.

DISCIPLE: Lord, this is true. I beg You, let it be done to me as You have said. May Your truth teach me. May it defend me and lead me to ultimate salvation. May I be free from evil passions and lawless love. With my heart set free, I will walk with You.

CHRIST: In truth, I will teach you what is right and pleasing in My eyes.[3] Recall your sins with great sorrow and displeasure and, whatever good deeds you may have done, think nothing of yourself. Remember that you are a sinner trapped and chained by many passions. In yourself you tend always to emptiness. You quickly fail and are overcome. You are rapidly disturbed and overthrown. You have nothing to boast about, but many things about which to be ashamed, for you are much weaker than you realize.

Do not regard anything you have done as being important. Do not let anything seem great, valuable or admirable to you. Nothing is worthy of respect, nothing eminent, praiseworthy or desirable except that which is eternal. Let your one and only joy be in the truth, and let your own miserable unworthiness always upset you. Nothing should be more feared, condemned and rejected than your own sins and vices. These should cause you more distress than if you lost everything. Some do not live obediently before Me[4] but, inspired by curiosity and arrogance, they wish to know My secrets and to discover the great mysteries of God, while ignoring the salvation of their own souls. When I refuse this, some people, because of their pride and inquisitiveness, often fall into great temptations and sins.

Stand in awe of God's decrees[5] and fear the vengeance of Almighty God.[6] Do not be so arrogant as to explore the ways of the Most High, but rather examine yourself. See how greatly you have sinned, and how much good you have neglected. Some pursue their devotion solely through books, pictures and other outward signs and illustrations. Some have Me on their lips, but few in their hearts.[7] There are others who are intellectually enlightened and have pure hearts and long for the things of heaven. These are reluctant to listen to worldly affairs, and resent having to meet their bodily needs. They completely understand the words of the Spirit of Truth within them.[8] For He teaches them to reject earthly things and to love heavenly things; to forsake this world and long for heaven.

FIVE

On the amazing effect of divine love

DISCIPLE: O heavenly Father of my Lord Jesus Christ, may Your name be blessed for ever, for You have seen fit to think of me, the poorest of Your servants. Father of all mercies and God of all consolation,[1] I thank You that, unworthy as I am, You sometimes revive me with Your consolation. Blessing and honour be to You, with Your only begotten Son and with the Holy Spirit, the Comforter, now and through all eternity. You are my glory[2] and the joy of my heart,[3] for You are my help and my refuge in the day of trouble.[4]

But now my love is weak and my goodness imperfect, so that I have great need of Your strength and comfort. So I pray, visit me often, and teach me in Your holy laws. Release me from evil and perverse passions and heal my heart from disorderly emotions; so that, healed and cleansed in spirit, I may grow more able to love, strong to endure and constant in perseverance.

Love is a mighty power, a total and immense good. Love alone lifts every burden and makes the rough places smooth.[5] It carries every hardship as if it were nothing and makes all bitterness sweet and acceptable. The love of Jesus is wonderful and inspires us to noble actions. It encourages us always to desire perfection. Love yearns for higher things and is not held back by worthless things. Love wants to be free and a stranger to worldly desires, lest its inner vision become dimmed, and lest worldly self-interest restrain it or bad luck leave it behind. Nothing is sweeter than love; nothing is stronger, nothing higher, nothing broader, nothing more pleasing, nothing larger or better in heaven or on earth. For love is born of God[6] and lies only in God, above all created things.

Love flies, runs and jumps for joy. It is free and unlimited. Love gives all for all, abiding in One who is higher than all things, from whom all goodness flows and emerges. Love is not concerned with gifts, but looks to the giver of all good gifts. Love knows no bounds, strongly transcends all barriers. Love feels no burdens, ignores hard work and aims at things beyond its powers. Love sees nothing as impossible, for it feels able to achieve all things.[7] So love can do great things. It is effective in its tasks, whereas those who lack love faint and fail.

Love is vigilant and, while it rests, it never sleeps. When weary, it is not exhausted; imprisoned, it is never in chains.[8] Disturbed, it is never afraid. It is a living flame and a burning light. It moves upward and overcomes every obstacle. Those who love God recognize the sound of His voice. The burning love of the soul cries out to the ears of God: 'My God and my love. You are mine and I am Yours.'

A PRAYER

O Lord, deepen Your love in me so that I may learn, in my own heart, how good it is to love; to be melted and to plunge myself into Your love. Let Your love possess and lift me above myself and to an enthusiasm and awe beyond imagining. Let me sing the song of love.[9] Let me follow You, my beloved, to the heights; let my soul be drained in Your praise, celebrating love. Let me love You more than myself, and myself only for Your own sake. Let me love all those who truly love You and the law of love, which shines out from Your commands.

Love is fast, pure, tender, joyful and satisfying. Love is strong, patient, faithful, wise, tolerant, energetic and never self-serving.[10] For when someone is self-serving, they give up love. Love is attentive, humble and righteous. Love is not capricious or sentimental, nor is it obsessed with superficial things. It is sensible, honest, reliable, quiet and restrained in all ways. Love is submissive and obedient to Superiors, mean and contemptible in its own sight, but devoted and grateful to God. It trusts and hopes in Him, even when there is no sweetness of joy. For no one can live in love without suffering,

Whoever is not willing to endure everything and stand firmly by the will of the Beloved is not worthy to be called a lover. Love must freely accept every hardship and bitterness for the sake of the Beloved, and in adversity must never desert Him.

SIX

On demonstrating true love

CHRIST: My child, you are not yet a brave and wise lover.
DISCIPLE: Why Lord?
CHRIST: Because, as soon as you face a little trouble, you give up what you have started and desperately seek consolation. A brave lover stands firm in temptation, and ignores the subtle arguments of the Devil. He is as true to Me in adversity as in prosperity.[1]

A wise lover respects not so much the gift of the lover, as the love of the giver. The affection is appreciated more than the gift, but every gift is valued less than the Beloved. A worthy lover is not content with the gift, but desires Me above all gifts. So if sometimes you do not feel that devotion to Me and My Saints that you desire, all is not lost. The good and sweet affection which you sometimes enjoy is the result of My grace in you and is a foretaste of your heavenly habitation. Do not rely on it too much, because it comes and goes. It is a valuable sign of virtue and merit, if you fight against recurring evil thoughts and reject scornfully the proposals of the Devil.

Do not be disturbed by strange impulses, wherever they come from. Stick boldly to your purpose and focus your proper objective on God alone.[2] If you are sometimes caught up in ecstasy, it is no illusion, but then you quickly return to your normal trivial thoughts. For these are involuntary, not deliberate, and as long as they do not please you, they can be turned to your gain and not your loss.

You can be sure that the old Enemy is working by every means possible to frustrate your desire for good, and to entice you away from every spiritual exercise and devotion: from the veneration of the Saints, from the devout consideration of My Passion, from beneficial examination of your sins, from the guarding of your heart, and from the determination to grow in holiness.

The Devil imposes many evil thoughts to discourage you, and draws you away from spiritual reading and prayer. He despises humble confession and, if he could, he would make you give up Holy Communion. Do not listen to him or believe in him, however often he tries to ensnare you. Accuse him of it when he suggests evil and unholy things. Say to him, 'Out of my sight, Satan,[3] be ashamed, miserable wretch. You are really foul to speak of these things. Away with you, most evil of liars. You shall have no place with me. Jesus will be with me like a mighty warrior and you will be confounded.[4] I would rather die and suffer any torture than agree with you. Keep silent and hold your tongue. I will not listen to you any longer, however often you pester me.' 'The Lord is my light and my salvation; whom shall I fear?'[5] 'Though an army encamp against me, my heart shall not fear.'[6] 'O Lord, my Rock and my Redeemer.'[7]

Fight like a good soldier,[8] and if weakness leads you to fall sometimes, recover great strength and put your trust in My more abundant grace. Also, be on your guard against conceit and self-loving. This can lead many into error, and sometimes causes complacency and almost incurable blindness of heart. Let the overthrowing of the proud, who trusted in their own strength, be a warning to you, and keep you perpetually humble.

SEVEN

On grace concealed under humility

CHRIST: My child, it is safer and better for you to hide the grace of devotion. Do not boast about it, do not speak frequently about it, and do not think much about it. It is better to think very humbly of yourself, and to fear that this grace has been granted to someone who is unworthy of it. Never rely much on feelings, for they may be quite quickly changed into their opposite. When you rejoice in grace, consider how sad and needy you are without it. Progress in the spiritual life depends not so much on enjoying consoling grace, as on accepting its withdrawal with humility, resignation and patience, and without growing weary in prayer or neglecting other acts of devotion. To the best of your ability and understanding do willingly whatever lies in your power and do not neglect your life of prayer because of dryness or anxiety.

There are many who become impatient or lazy when things do not go the way they want them to. But our life is not always under our control.[1] It is up to God to offer consolation when He wishes, as much as He wishes, and to whom He wishes, just as He pleases and no more. Some careless people have brought ruin on themselves in their experience of devotion by attempting things beyond their powers, and ignoring the measure of their own insignificance by following the promptings of their heart rather than rational judgement. Because they presumed greater things than God expects of them, they soon lost His grace. These souls, who sought to build their nest beyond the clouds,[2] became needy and wretched outcasts. Thus they were brought low and into poverty, so that they might learn not to fly with their own wings, but to put themselves under My wings.[3] Those

who are still new and untested in the ways of the Lord can easily be deceived and lost, unless they are guided by wise advice.

If they follow their own ideas rather than trust other experienced people, their end will be perilous, unless they are willing
to be weaned away from their own conceits. For those who are
wise in their own conceit[4] rarely accept with humility the guidance of others. A little knowledge and understanding tempered
by humility is better than a great treasury of knowledge linked
to self-satisfaction. It is better to have a few talents than many,
which can lead to conceit. Those who surrender to happiness,
forgetful of their former poverty, are very unwise. For they forget also the pure reverence for the Lord which is frightened to
lose the grace which has been given. Nor is someone wise who,
in times of adversity, gives in to despair and does not trust in Me.

Those who feel secure in times of peace can often be discouraged and afraid in times of war. If you took care to stay humble
and modest about yourself, and to direct and control your
mind in moderation,[5] you would not so easily fall into danger
and disgrace. When the devotional Spirit is aflame in you, you
will be well advised to consider how you will behave when that
light leaves you. When this does happen, remember that this
light, which I have temporarily withdrawn, is a warning to you
and is for My glory[6] and will return one day.

Such testing is more often beneficial than if all went well
with you and in accordance with your wishes. For our worthiness is not to be measured by the visions and comforts we may
enjoy, nor by knowledge of the Scriptures, nor by being lifted
to an elevated position. It is, rather, measured by being steeped
in humility and filled with the love of God, by simple, regular
and sincere seeking for God's glory, by the low esteem and dep-
recation of ourselves,[7] and by preferring to be despised and
humiliated rather than the great honours that others receive.

EIGHT

On humility in the sight of God

DISCIPLE: 'Let me take it upon myself to speak to the Lord, I who am dust and ashes.'[1] If I think of myself as anything more than that, You confront me, and my sins, which I cannot refute, bear true witness against me. But if I humble myself and admit my nothingness; if I reject all my self-esteem and reduce myself to the dust that I really am, then Your grace will come to me, and Your light will come into my heart. So the last trace of self-esteem will be swallowed up in the depth of my own nothingness, and vanish for ever. In this way You reveal my true self to me – what I am, what I have been and what I have become – because in myself I am nothing and I did not realize it. By myself, I am nothing and am all weakness. But if, for a moment, You look on me, I become strong once again and am filled with new joy. It amazes me how quickly You lift up and enfold me with Your grace, who on my own would fall into the depths.

It is Your love that achieves this, guiding and supporting me freely in my many needs, guarding me from terrible dangers and, as I honestly confess, saving me from endless evils. Since, by pernicious self-love, I had lost myself,[2] now by seeking to love You alone I have found both You and myself. By that love I have humbled myself into total nothingness. Sweetest Lord, You treat me much better than I deserve, and above all that I dare to hope or pray for.

O my blessed Lord God, I am not worthy of any blessings, yet Your kindness and endless goodness never stop benefiting even those who are ungrateful[3] and have strayed far from You. Turn our hearts to You,[4] so that we may be grateful, humble and dedicated. For You are our salvation, our power and our strength.

NINE

Everything relates to God as our last end

CHRIST: My child, if you desire to be truly blessed, I must be your highest and final end. Too often your affections are wrongly focused on yourself or other creatures. But, if they are fixed on Me, they will be cleansed. When you seek yourself in anything you at once become discouraged and desolate. So refer everything to Me, for it is I who have given everything to you. Realize that everything emerges from the supreme Good,[1] because they must all return to Me as their Creator.

Draw the water of life[2] from Me, as from a living fountain, small and great, rich and poor alike. Those who freely and gladly serve Me will receive grace upon grace.[3] But whoever seeks to rejoice in anything other than Me,[4] or to delight in some personal benefit, will not be grounded in true joy or be free of heart.[5] They will be hindered and frustrated in many ways. So ascribe nothing good to yourself or anyone else, but attribute everything to God, without whom you have nothing. I have given everything and I desire that everything will return to Me again. I shall demand a grateful and exact account.

It is this truth which puts to rout all false glory. If heavenly grace and true love enter in, there will be no envy or meanness of heart, nor will self-love predominate. For God's love conquers everything[6] and increases every power of the soul. If you are really wise, you will rejoice and hope in Me alone; for no one is good except God alone.[7] He is to be praised above all and to be blessed in all.

TEN

On despising the world and the joy of serving God

DISCIPLE: Lord, I cannot keep silent. I will speak once more. I will say to my God, my Lord and my King, who lives on high, 'O how abundant is Your goodness that You have laid up for those who fear You.'[1] But what are You to those who love You? What are You to those who serve You with their whole heart? The contemplation of Yourself is endless sweetness, which You lavish on those who love You. The great demonstration of Your love is shown in that, when I had no being, You created me. When I went astray, You brought me back to Your service and taught me to love You.[2]

O source of eternal love, what can I say of You? How can I forget You, who have consented to remember me,[3] even after I was corrupted and lost? The mercy You have shown to Your servant is beyond all my expectations. You have given grace and friendship beyond all that I deserve. What return can I make to You for this grace?[4] For it is not given to all of us to surrender everything, to renounce the things of the world and enter into the Religious Life. All creation is bound to serve You, so is it a wonderful thing that I should serve You? It should not seem much to me that I should serve You, but it is a great and wonderful thing for me that You are willing to accept into Your service one so poor and unworthy and be willing to count me among Your beloved servants.

All that I have is Yours, including myself.[5] But it is You who serve me rather than I serving You. You created heaven and earth for the use of humanity, and they await Your pleasure and obey Your laws every day. And this is very little since You have appointed Your angels to minister to us.[6] But above all this, You come down Yourself to serve us and have promised us the gift of Yourself.

What return can I make for all these endless gifts? If only I could serve You faithfully all the days of my life![7] If only I could offer You proper service even for one single day! For You alone are worthy of all service, honour and everlasting praise.[8] You are truly my God, and I am Your poor servant, bound to serve with all my ability, nor should I ever tire of praising You. It is my wish and desire that I ask You to supply in me whatever is lacking.

It is a great honour and glory to serve You and to despise everything else for Your sake. Great grace will be given to those who have entered willingly into Your most holy service. Those who for Your love have renounced all the delights of the flesh will discover the delectable consolations of the Holy Spirit.[9] Those who enter on the narrow way[10] and put aside all worldly interests for Your name's sake will win true freedom of mind.

O gracious and joyful service of God, in which we are made truly free and holy! O sacred state of devout service, which makes us equal to the Angels, pleasing to God, terrifying to devils and an example to all faithful people! O most lovely and desirable service, in which we receive the reward of the supreme God and gain the joy that lasts for ever!

ELEVEN

*The desires of the heart need to be
examined and disciplined*

CHRIST: My child, you have still many things to learn.

DISCIPLE: Lord, what are these?

CHRIST: You must shape your desires in accordance with My will,[1] and not love yourself, but be a disciple of My wishes. Desires often inflame you, and violently drive you forward. But reflect on whether you are moved most by your self-interest or by My honour. If I am the reason, you will be satisfied with whatever I shall decide. But if your hidden motive is self-interest, this will be an obstacle and a burden to you.

So take care not to depend excessively on any preconceived desire without asking My advice, in case you come to regret or be displeased with what at first satisfied you, and for which you were very enthusiastic. Not every feeling that seems good should be acted upon at once, nor should every feeling that runs contrary to your inclinations be rejected immediately. It is sometimes necessary to restrain even your good intentions and endeavours, in case by too much enthusiasm your mind becomes distracted, or by lack of discipline you offend others, or you suddenly become confused and upset by the opposition of others.

You must bravely and forcibly resist your sensual appetite, ignoring what the body likes or dislikes, and struggle to subdue the unwilling flesh to the spirit.[2] For, unless it is obedient in everything, it must be corrected and brought under control. It must learn to be content with little, to take pleasure in simple things and not to complain of any hardship.

TWELVE

On gaining patience and resisting evil desires

DISCIPLE: O Lord God, I know that endurance is necessary above all else.[1] For in this life there are many trials. However earnestly I seek peace, I cannot escape struggle and sorrow.[2]

CHRIST: This is true, My child. But it is My desire that you do not try to find somewhere free of troubles and temptations. It is better to seek a peace that endures, even when you are disturbed by various temptations and tested by great adversity.[3] If you say that you cannot endure much, how will you endure the fires of purgatory?[4] Always choose the lesser of two evils. For God's sake try to endure patiently all the ills of this life so that you may escape everlasting punishment. Do you think that people in this world suffer little or nothing? Ask the richest people, and you will find that is not the case.

But, you may reply, they enjoy many pleasures and follow their own desires. In that way they make light of their afflictions. But even if they enjoy what they desire, how long will it last? The rich of this world will be dispersed like smoke[5] and no memory of their past pleasures will remain. But even while they are living, they do not enjoy them without bitterness, weariness and fear. For the very things from which they derive their pleasures often carry with them the seeds of sorrow. And this is only right, for having sought and followed pleasures to excess, they cannot enjoy them without shame and bitterness. How short-lived and false, how disorderly and ignoble are all these pleasures! Yet such people are besotted and blind, so that, like dumb animals, they bring death to their souls by the passing enjoyments of this corruptible world! My child, do not follow your lusts or be self-willed.[6] Delight in the Lord and He will grant you your heart's desire.[7]

If you wish to taste real pleasure and receive the fullness of My consolation, realize that your blessing will come from despising worldly things and resisting low desires. In this way you will gain abundant blessings. The more you withdraw yourself from worldly comforts, the sweeter and stronger consolation you will find in Me. But you will not find these all at once, or without sorrow, work and effort. Old habits will be obstacles but, through better habits, they will be overcome.[8] The body will complain, but a fervent spirit can discipline it. That Ancient Serpent[9] will provoke and disturb you, but he will be put to flight by prayer. By profitable work you close the wide path through which he comes to attack you.

THIRTEEN

*On humble obedience after the
example of Christ*

CHRIST: My child, whoever tries to break away from obedience, leaves grace behind. Those who seek personal privileges lose those which are common to everyone. When someone is reluctant to obey a Superior freely and willingly, it is a sign that the lower nature is not yet under control, but often rebels and complains. So, if you wish to subdue your lower nature, learn to obey your Superior promptly. For the external enemy is more easily conquered if the inner being is not broken down. When you are not in harmony with the Spirit, there is no enemy more wicked or troublesome for the soul than yourself. If you are to triumph over flesh and blood, you must have real contempt for yourself. You are not willing to surrender your will to others because you are still full of self-love.

Is it such a great thing for you, who are only dust and nothing,[1] to submit yourself to another for God's sake, when I, the Almighty and the Most High, who created everything out of nothing, humbly submitted Myself to humanity for your sake?[2] I became the humblest and least of all, so that through My humility you might overcome your pride. You, who are but dust, must learn to obey. You, who are earth and clay, must learn to humble yourself and to grovel before the feet of all. Learn to restrain your desires and surrender yourself to total obedience.

Turn your anger on yourself, and do not allow swollen pride to remain in you. Show yourself to be so submissive and humble that everyone may walk on you and trample over you, like the mud in the streets.[3] You worthless person, what right have you to complain? What can you, an unclean sinner, reply to anyone who castigates you when you have so often offended God and so many times deserved hell? But I have spared you,[4] for your soul was precious to Me, so that you may know My love and always be grateful for My kindness. Also, accept patiently any contempt laid on you in order that you might continuously give yourself to true obedience and humility.

FOURTEEN

*On the need to consider God's secret judgements
and not to rejoice in goodness*

DISCIPLE: Your judgements thunder against me, Lord. My bones tremble and shake with fear, and my soul is greatly frightened. I stand awestruck, reflecting that the very heavens are not innocent in Your sight.[1] If You found Your Angels at fault[2] and You did not spare them,[3] what can be my fate? Even the stars fall from heaven.[4] What then of me who am but dust? People with praiseworthy actions have fallen into the pit, and I have seen those who have been fed with the bread of Angels[5] guzzling pig's food.

Lord, if you withdraw Yourself, there can be no holiness. If You cease to guide, no wisdom will help. If You cease to defend us, no courage can sustain us. If You do not guard us, no purity is safe. No watchfulness of our own can save us unless Your holy direction protects us.[6] For if You abandon us, we drown and perish.[7] But if You come to us, we are raised up and live again. We are unreliable, unless You strengthen us. We are cold and dull unless You inflame us with enthusiasm.

How humble and insignificant I am! If there is any good in me it is as nothing. Lord, I submit myself in all humility to Your mysterious judgements.[8] O immeasurable greatness, I acknowledge my total nothingness. O impassable ocean! Now I see myself as totally and wholly nothing! Where can pride conceal itself now? Where is my previous confidence in my virtue now? All my empty conceits are swallowed up in the depths of Your judgements upon me.

What is all flesh in Your eyes?[9] Can the clay boast against Him who shaped it?[10] Can anyone who is truly subject to God be puffed up with vain boasting?[11] The whole world cannot lift up someone whom the truth has made subject to itself, nor can anyone who has put all hope in God be moved by the words of those flatterers. Even those who speak like this are nothing. They will pass away with the sound of their own words, but the truth of the Lord stands fast for ever.[12]

FIFTEEN

*How we should act and speak
in relation to our desires*

CHRIST: My child, let your prayer always be: 'Lord, if it be Your will, let it be so.[1] Lord, if this is good and beneficial, give me grace to use it to Your glory. But if it harms or hurts my soul's health, then I pray take this desire out of my mind.' Not every desire comes from the Holy Spirit, even if it seems right and good. It is frequently hard to decide whether a desire springs from good or from evil motives or whether it arises out of your own impulses. Many who at first seemed to be led by the Holy Spirit are finally deceived.

So whatever the mind considers beneficial is only to be desired and sought in the fear of God and with humility. Above all, entrust everything to Me, and commit yourself totally to Me, saying: 'Lord, You know what is best; let everything be in accordance with Your will. Grant what You will, as much as You will, and when You will. Do with me as You will and is best pleasing to You and is most to Your glory. I am in Your hands: guide me according to Your will. I am your servant[2] and I am ready for anything. I do not wish to live for myself, but only for You. How I wish I could serve You suitably and perfectly!'

A PRAYER THAT THE WILL OF
GOD MAY BE DONE

DISCIPLE: Most gracious Jesus, grant me Your grace, I pray. Let it live in me and work in me[3] and stay in me until the end.

Grant me the will and desire to do always what is most pleasing and acceptable to You. Let Your will be mine and let my will always follow and be conformed totally to Your own. May my will be at one with You, and unable to do anything other than what You like or dislike. May I die to all things in this world, and for Your sake love to be despised and unknown. Above all let me rest in You[4] so that my heart may find peace in You alone. For You are the real peace of the heart, its proper resting place, and away from You all is hard and restless. I will live and take my rest[5] in the real peace, which is in You, the final, supreme and everlasting Good. Amen.

SIXTEEN

How true comfort is found in God alone

DISCIPLE: Whatever I wish or hope for in consolation, I do not expect to find now, but later. For, if I were to enjoy all the pleasures of the world and were able to experience all its delights,[1] they would certainly pass away. So my soul can never find total satisfaction or complete refreshment except in God alone. He is the comfort of the poor and the defender of the humble. Be patient, my soul; wait for the completion of God's promise and you will enjoy the richness of His goodness in heaven. But if you long excessively after the good things of life, you will lose those of heaven and eternity.[2] So put to good use the things of this world, but only desire the things that are eternal. The things of this world will never satisfy you because you were not created for the simple enjoyment of them.[3]

If you enjoyed everything that exists, this would not in itself bring you blessing and happiness, for all true joy and blessing lies in God alone, who is the Creator of all things. Those who foolishly love this world cannot see or admire this sort of happiness. It is only sought by the good and faithful servants of Christ. They are those who are spiritual and pure in heart,[4] whose thoughts are on heaven and sometimes enjoy a foretaste of it. All human consolation is empty and brief. Blessing and true comfort is received inwardly from the truth. A devout person always carries Jesus the Comforter in the heart and says to Him, 'Lord Jesus, stay with me everywhere and at all times; let this be my comfort, to be ready and willing to go without all earthly comfort. And if Your consolation is missing may Your holy will and just judgement of my life be my greatest comfort. For You will not always be angry nor will You condemn me for ever.'[5]

SEVENTEEN

How we must put our whole trust in God

CHRIST: My child, let My will be your guide. I know what is best for you. Your understanding is human and your judgement is affected by your personal concerns.

DISCIPLE: Lord, what You say is true. Your concern will order my life better than I can myself. Those who do not place their anxiety on You[1] will be very insecure. Lord, keep my will steadfast and true to You. Do with me whatever You please, for everything is good which comes to me through Your will. If You want me to be in darkness, blessed be Your name. If it is light, blessed be Your name. If You grant me comfort, blessed be Your name. If You wish to test me, blessed be Your name for ever.

CHRIST: My child, if you wish to walk with Me may this be your inclination. Be just as ready to suffer as to be happy, be as willing to be poor and needy as to enjoy wealth and prosperity.

DISCIPLE: Lord, I will accept gladly whatever You will send to me. I will accept gladly from Your hand both good and evil,[2] sweet and bitter, joy and sorrow, and I will thank You whatever happens to me. Lord, just keep me from all sin and I will fear neither death nor hell.[3] I ask that You do not reject me for ever,[4] nor remove my name from the book of life.[5] Then whatever trials afflict me can do me no harm.

EIGHTEEN

*How we must follow patiently Christ's
example in bearing sufferings*

CHRIST: My child, I came down from heaven for your salvation.[1] I took your sorrows upon Myself, not because I had to, but out of pure love, so that you might learn patience and accept without complaint all the troubles of the world. From the moment of My birth until My death on the Cross, I had always to endure sufferings.[2] I suffered the loss of all worldly goods. Many accusations were brought against Me. When I was insulted and shamed, I accepted it gently. In return for blessing, I received ingratitude; for miracles, blasphemies; and for My teaching, rebukes.

DISCIPLE: Lord, during Your life You were patient, especially in fulfilling Your Father's commands. So it is fitting that I, a miserable sinner, should patiently bear the burdens of this corruptible life, according to Your will and for the salvation of my soul, as long as it will be Your will. For even though this present life is hard, by Your grace it is made full of merit. By Your example and the lives of Your Saints it is made easier and happier for the weak. Its consolations are richer than under the old law, when the gates of heaven were shut and the path to it dark, so that few cared to enter the Kingdom of Heaven. And even those who in former days were righteous and to be saved could not enter the Kingdom of Heaven until Your Passion and the Atonement of Your holy death had taken place.

What endless gratitude is due to You for showing to me and to all faithful people the true and holy way to Your everlasting kingdom! Your life is our way, and by holy persistence we will travel towards You, our crown and our encouragement. Lord, if You had not gone ahead of us and shown us the way, who could follow You?[3] How many would have stayed behind, a long way back, if they did not have Your great example as their guide? We are cold and careless even though we have heard Your teaching and Your powerful acts. What would happen to us if we did not have Your light as a guide?[4]

NINETEEN

On accepting injuries and the proof of patience

CHRIST: My child, what is it you are saying? Stop complaining and reflect on My sufferings and those of My Saints. You have not yet resisted to the point of shedding your blood.[1] Your troubles are but small in comparison with those who have suffered so much, whose temptations were strong, whose trials were severe and who were proved and tested in very many ways.[2] Remember the much greater sufferings of others, so that you may more easily bear your own small troubles. If they do not seem small to you, your impatience may be the cause; and whether they are small or great, try to accept them patiently.

The better you prepare yourself to accept suffering, the more wisely you will accept it, and the greater will be your merit. You will accept everything more easily if your heart and mind are properly prepared. Do not say, 'I cannot tolerate it from this person, nor will I put up with these things. A great injury has been done to me and accusations made about things I have never considered. But I will gladly accept it from another person as far as I regard it as something to be tolerated.' Such thoughts are foolish, for if you think only of the person who has injured you and the wrongs you suffer, you ignore the benefits of patience and Him who rewards it.

You are not really patient if you only put up with what you think you should, and only from those you like. A really patient person does not consider those who test them, be they a superior or an equal, or an inferior person, or a good and holy person, or a perverse and wicked one. But however great or frequent the trials that beset you, and from whatever source they come, gladly accept them as from the hand of God and it is all gain.

If you wish for victory, always be ready for battle. You cannot win the crown of patience without a struggle.[3] If you refuse to suffer, you decline the crown. If you desire the crown, fight bravely and endure patiently. No rest is won without hard work. There can be no victory without a battle.

DISCIPLE: Lord, that which is impossible to me by my nature make possible to me by Your grace. You know how little I can bear, and how quickly I become discouraged by small adversities. I pray You to make every test lovely and desirable for Your name's sake. Suffering and pain for Your sake are so beneficial to the health of my soul.

TWENTY

On confessing our weakness and the trials of life

DISCIPLE: Lord, I confess my sinfulness and acknowledge my weakness.[1] Often it is a little thing which defeats and troubles me. I decide to act boldly, but when I am disturbed by a little temptation, I am in a tight corner. A very petty thing can lead to a strong temptation; and when I think I am safe, I am almost knocked over by a light breeze.

Lord, look on my lowness and weakness, for You know everything. Have mercy on me and lift me up from the mire, so that I may not stick fast in it[2] nor stay defeated. Frequently, this is what defeats and beats me down before You: that I am liable to fall and am so weak in resisting my passions. And although I do not always totally give in to them, yet their assaults trouble and distress me, so that I am tired of living constantly in conflict. My weakness is clear to me, for evil fantasies rush in more quickly than they depart.

Most mighty God of Israel, zealous lover of souls, I ask You to remember the toil and grief of Your servant and to support me in all that I do. Strengthen me with heavenly courage lest my old and wicked enemy, the flesh, which is not yet totally subject to the spirit, prevail and gain the upper hand. For whilethere is breath in me in this troublesome life, I must fight against it. What a sad life it is where trials and sorrows never end, and where all things are full of snares and enemies. For when one test or temptation departs another takes its place.[3] Even while the battle rages, other unnumbered and unexpected troubles arise.

How can we love life, when it holds such bitterness and produces so many sorrows and abuses? How, then, can it be called life, which spawns such a great amount of pain and death? Yet it is loved and many find great delight in it. The world is often blamed for its falseness and vanity, but it is not easily given up. The desires of the body exert a strong control. Some things make us love the world; other things make us hate it. All that panders to the appetites, or entices the eyes and all the arrogance of life,[4] draws us to love the world. But the pains and sorrows that rightly follow cause us to hate and be tired of it.

It is sad that a perverted idea of pleasure conquers the mind and surrenders to the world, and enjoys lying among the brambles.[5] It has neither seen nor tasted the sweetness of God[6] and the inner joy of holiness. But those who perfectly despise the world, and study to live under God's holy law, know something of that heavenly sweetness promised to all who sincerely leave the world behind. They see very clearly how the world goes astray, and how grievously it is deceived.

TWENTY-ONE

How we must rest in God above all His gifts

DISCIPLE: O my soul, rest always in the Lord above all things and in all things, for He is the everlasting rest of the Saints.

A PRAYER

Most dear and loving Jesus, let me rest in You above all created things;[1] above health and beauty; above all glory and honour; above all power and grandeur; above all knowledge and skill; above all fame and praise; above all sweetness and consolation; above all hope and promise; above all merit and desire; above all the gifts and favours that You can award and shower upon us; above all joy and celebration that the mind can conceive and know; above Angels and Archangels and all the hosts of heaven; above all things visible and invisible and everything that is not Yourself, O my God.

O Lord my God, You transcend all things; You alone are Most High, most mighty, most sufficient and complete, most sweet and comforting. You alone are most full of beauty and glory, in whom all good things in their perfection exist, both now and ever have been and ever will be. Therefore everything that You can give me is too small and unsatisfying except Yourself, or that which You can reveal and promise me of Yourself unless I can see and fully possess You. For my heart cannot rest nor be wholly content until it rests in You,[2] and rises above all Your gifts and creatures.

O Lord Jesus Christ, spouse of the soul,[3] lover of purity and Lord of creation, who will give me wings of perfect liberty so that I may fly to You and be at rest?[4] When shall I be set free and taste Your sweetness?[5] O Lord my God, when shall I become

totally absorbed in You, so that for love of You I may no longer
be conscious of myself but only of You, in a way not known to
many and beyond all perception and analysis? But now I mourn
and carry my unhappy load with grief, for in this vale of sorrows
many evils occur which frequently disturb, sadden and darken
my path. They often obstruct and distract, entice and entangle
me, so that I cannot approach You freely, nor yet enjoy the sweet
embrace which You prepare for the souls of the blessed.

O Jesus, brightness of eternal glory, and comfort of the pilgrim soul, hear my cry and look on my total desolation. Words
fail me in Your presence; may my silence speak for me. How
long will My Lord delay His coming? Lord, come to me, the
poor and small thing that I am, and bring me joy. Stretch out
Your hand and save me from all misery and pain. Come Lord,
come,[6] for no day or hour is happy without You. Without You
my table has no guest, for You alone are my joy. Sadness is my
due and I am like someone imprisoned and loaded with chains
until You revive me with the light of Your presence and, as my
friend, show Your face.[7] Let others look for whatever they wish
apart from You, but nothing can ever, or will ever, give me joy
except You alone, my God, my hope and my eternal salvation.
I will not keep silent, nor cease from urgent prayer, until Your
grace returns and my heart leaps at the sound of Your voice.

CHRIST: See, I am here. I have come at your call. Your tears
and your soul's desire, your humiliation and penitence of heart,
have moved Me to come to you.

DISCIPLE: Lord, I have called for You and longed for You. I
am ready to surrender everything for Your sake, who first
moved me to look for You. Blessed be Your name, O Lord, for
Your goodness to Your servant according to the riches of Your
mercy.[8] What more can Your servant say, Lord? Ever mindful
of my own wickedness and unworthiness, I can only humble
myself completely in Your presence. For among the wonders of
earth and heaven, nothing can compare with You.[9]

All Your works are good. Your judgements are true[10] and by
Your providence You rule over everything. Praise and glory be
to You, O Wisdom of the Father! Let my soul, my lips and all
creation join in Your blessing and Your praise.

TWENTY-TWO

On recalling God's many blessings

DISCIPLE: Open my heart, O Lord, to understand Your law and teach me to live according to Your commandments.[1] Let me know Your will and let me devoutly reflect on all Your many blessings so that hereafter I may give to You proper and worthy thanks. I realize and confess that I am utterly unable to give You proper gratitude, even for the smallest of the many blessings You give me. For I am less than the least of all Your gifts. When I think of Your endless generosity, I faint before its magnitude.

Whatever powers of the soul or the body we possess, outwardly or inwardly, natural or supernatural, are Your own gifts. They proclaim the richness of the loving and good God from whom we receive all good gifts.[2] All gifts are Yours, whether they are many or few, and without You we have nothing. So those who have received endless gifts should not, for that reason, boast of any merits or exalt themselves above other human beings, nor despise those who are not so richly endowed. For the greater and better someone is, the less they will attribute to themselves, and the more humbly and devoutly give thanks to God. Those who hold themselves in humble esteem and consider themselves unworthy are more fitted to receive God's greatest gifts.

Someone who has not gained many gifts should not, for that reason, be disappointed or envious of those who have been given much more. It is better if they turn to You and praise Your goodness. For Your gifts are given generously, freely and willingly, without any respect of persons.[3] All good things come from You, so You are to be praised in all things.[4] You alone know what is fitting for each person to receive, and it is not for us to judge why one has less and another more. You alone can weigh the merits of each one.

O Lord God, I count it a great mercy not to have many of those gifts which, in the eyes of others, seem to be praiseworthy and admirable. For those who recognize their own poverty and inferiority should not be sad, sorry or dejected because of that. It is better that they should take comfort and be glad that You, O God, have chosen the poor, the humble, the despised in this world to be Your own familiar friends[5] and servants. Your Apostles are themselves examples of this and You made them princes of the whole earth.[6] Yet they lived in this world without complaining, being so humble, simple and without malice and deceit that they were glad to suffer reproaches for Your name's sake[7] and they embraced readily what the world seeks to avoid.

Nothing should give so much joy to anyone who loves You and receives Your blessings as that they should see Your holy will and good pleasure being fulfilled in them according to Your eternal purpose. They should be so greatly comforted by and content with this that they would be gladly seen as the least of people, in the same way as some might wish to be seen as very great. They should be as peaceable and content in the end as in the beginning.[8] They should be as willing to be anonymous, despised and outcast with no reputation as to be honoured and exalted among the famous. It is Your will and the honour of Your name that must come before everything else. This will bring greater comfort and richer pleasure than all other benefits that have been or may be given.

TWENTY-THREE

On four things that bring peace

CHRIST: My child, I will now teach you the way of peace and true freedom.

DISCIPLE: Lord, teach me, please, I am eager to learn.

CHRIST: My child, do the will of others rather than your own.[1]

Always choose to possess less rather than more.[2]

Always take the lowest place and see yourself as less than others.[3]

Desire and pray always that God's will may be perfectly fulfilled in you.[4]

Those who observe these rules will come to enjoy peace and calmness of soul.

DISCIPLE: Lord, the whole secret of perfection lies in these few words of Yours. They are briefly put, but rich in meaning. If I could ever faithfully keep them, no trouble would distress me. For whenever I am anxious and weary, I find it is because I have strayed from Your teaching. All things are in Your power, and You always want to bring souls to perfection. Give me Your grace more fully. Help me to keep Your Word and move towards salvation.

A PRAYER AGAINST EVIL THOUGHTS

My Lord and my God, do not abandon me. Remember my needs, for many evil thoughts and terrible fears disturb my mind and frighten my soul. How shall I pass through them unhurt? How shall I break their power over me? You have said to me, 'I will go before you and will humble the proud.'[5] 'I will open the gates of the prison and reveal to you the hidden treasures and secrets of the ages.' O Lord, do as You have promised and let Your coming put to flight all evil thoughts. It is my hope and comfort that I can turn to You in all my troubles, put my trust in You, call upon You in my heart, and patiently wait for Your comfort.

A PRAYER FOR ENLIGHTENMENT

O merciful Jesus, send the brightness of Your light into my mind and banish all darkness from the sanctuary of my heart. Hold back many perverse thoughts and crush the temptations which surround me so violently. May Your strength be with me in the fight and overcome the seductive desires of the flesh, which rage in me like evil beasts. Bring peace by Your power[6] and let Your praises be sung in the temple of a pure heart. Command the winds and storm,[7] subdue the fury of the seas[8] and the blast of the north wind, and there will be great calm. Send out Your light and Your truth[9] to shine over the world; for until Your light illuminates my soul, I am just dull earth, formless and empty.[10] Pour out Your grace from above, and bathe my heart in the dew of heaven.[11] Send fresh springs of devotion to water the face of the earth[12] and produce good and perfect fruit. Inspire my mind, now burdened by my sins, and fix my whole desire on heavenly things. Then, having once tasted the sweetness of everlasting joys, I may turn with disgust from all the passing pleasures of this world. Release me and set free my heart from all dependence on the transitory consolation of evil things. None of them can offer true satisfaction or fulfil my desires. Unite me to Yourself by the unbreakable bonds of love. You alone can satisfy the souls who love You, and without You the world is worthless.

TWENTY-FOUR

On avoiding curiosity about other people's lives

CHRIST: My child, beware of curiosity and do not bother about empty matters.[1] What are they to you? Follow Me.[2] What concern is it of yours if someone is good or evil, or what anyone says or does? You will not be called to answer for others but you will definitely have to give an account of your own life.[3] Why meddle where you do not need to? I know the hearts of everyone,[4] and nothing under the sun is hidden from My knowledge. I know everyone's lives, their thoughts, their desires and their intentions. So trust yourself totally to My care and let your heart be at peace. Let those who are inquisitive trouble themselves as they like. Their words and deeds will recoil on their own heads. For no one can deceive Me.

Do not curry favour with powerful patrons, or seek fame, nor even the special affection of friends. All these things are distractions and fill the heart with uncertainty. If you will be careful to watch for My coming and throw open the door of your heart,[5] I will speak to you and reveal My secrets. Be ready, watch and pray.[6] Above all, be humble.

TWENTY-FIVE

On lasting peace of mind and true progress

CHRIST: I have said, 'Peace I leave with you; My peace I give to you. I do not give to you as the world gives.'[1] Everyone wants peace but they do not all seek the things that bring real peace. My peace is with the humble and gentle of heart[2] and depends on great patience. If you listen to Me and follow My words, you will find true peace.

DISCIPLE: What must I do, Lord?

CHRIST: Pay attention to your whole life, what you say and do. Direct all your efforts to the one purpose of pleasing Me. Seek and desire Myself alone.[3] Never pass rash judgements on the behaviour of others, and when you have not been asked your opinion, do not interfere. If you do as I tell you, you will rarely be troubled in mind. But do not imagine that you can avoid anxiety in this life, or that you will never experience emotional sorrow or physical pain, for true peace is only to be found in the state of eternal rest. So when you happen to experience no trouble, do not think that you have found true peace. Do not think all is well when no one opposes you. Nor should you consider that everything is perfect when everything happens as you want it. When you enjoy the grace of great devotion and sweetness, do not have a high opinion of yourself, or believe that you are God's favourite. For the true lover of holiness is not known by these things, nor is our spiritual progress dependent on such things.

DISCIPLE: Then on what does it depend, Lord?

CHRIST: On the total surrender of your heart to the will of God, not seeking to have your own way, either in big or small matters, or in time or eternity. If you will make this submission you will thank God with equal gladness both in good times and in bad. Then you will accept everything as from His hand with an untroubled mind. Be courageous, and have such an unshakeable faith that when spiritual consolation is withdrawn you may prepare your heart for even greater trials. Do not think it is unjust that you suffer so much, but confess that I am righteous in all My dealings and so praise My holy name. In so doing you will walk in the true and noble path of peace, and I will surely come to you again[4] and give you great joy.[5] Just think humbly of yourself, and I promise you the greatest peace[6] that is possible in this life.

TWENTY-SIX

On the excellence of an independent mind and the reward of humble prayer rather than reading

DISCIPLE: Lord, those who desire perfection must firstly keep the mind fixed on heavenly things at all times. By so doing they can pass through many troubles in a carefree way, not as those who lack the wisdom to realize the dangers around them, but in the strength of a free mind, unfettered by unnecessary attachment to worldly things.

Most loving God, I ask You to protect me so that I am not overcome by the cares of this life. Also, keep me from becoming a slave to my body's many needs, so that I do not become absorbed in its pleasures. Save me from all the pitfalls which afflict my soul, so that I may not be overwhelmed or crushed by them. I do not ask to be protected from those things that vain and worldly people pursue with such ardour, but rather from those miseries that so heavily weigh down and impede the soul of Your servant, who lies under the curse which is common to all mortals.[1] It is these miseries that prevent my soul from entering into the true freedom of the spirit whenever I want. My God, my ineffable delight, make all worldly pleasure bitter to me. It draws me away from the love of everlasting joys, and wickedly seduces me by promising the joys of the present. I pray that I may not be overwhelmed by flesh and blood.[2] Do not let the world and its passing glory deceive me, nor let the Devil and his cunning overthrow me. Give me strength to resist, patience to endure and constancy to persevere. Give me the rich graces of Your spirit rather than the pleasures of the world, and replace all worldly love with the love of Your name.

The soul of a fervent spirit resents giving attention to food, drink, clothing and other bodily needs. Let me use these things in moderation, and not be over-concerned about them.[3] It is wrong to ignore them, for nature calls us to meet those needs, but the law of holiness forbids us to crave useless luxuries, for then the body rebels against the spirit. I ask that Your hand may guide and rule me in all things so that moderation may be my rule at all times.

TWENTY-SEVEN

*How self-love is a great hindrance
to the highest good*

CHRIST: My child, you must give all for all and hold back nothing of yourself from Me. Understand that self-love does you more harm than anything else in the world. All things take your heart prisoner to a greater or lesser degree, in proportion to the love and regard you give to them.[1] If your love is pure, simple and controlled you will not be a slave of these things. Do not long after things which are not rightly yours, and possess nothing that hinders your spiritual progress or robs you of inner freedom. It is strange that you are not willing to trust yourself to Me with all your heart, together with everything that you may desire or enjoy.

Why wear yourself out with empty grief? Why impose needless anxieties on yourself? Trust in My kindness to you and you will experience no loss. If you want this or that thing, or to be here or there in order to suit your wishes or convenience, you will never be at rest or free from worry. There will always be something that does not please you, and everywhere you will find someone who opposes your wishes.

There is nothing to be gained by acquiring or increasing your possessions. Rather, it is better to be indifferent to such things, and wiping out the desire for them from your heart. These harmful desires consist not only in a love of wealth, but also in ambition for honours and empty praise. Remember that all these things fade away with the world. If we have no enthusiasm, it does not matter very much where we live and work, nor will we find lasting peace in outward affairs. Unless your life is built on firm foundations[2] and unless you stand firm in

My strength, you will hardly be able to amend your life. So whenever it occurs, seize the opportunity for self-surrender. You will discover the secret in what you have so far tried to avoid; indeed, you will find even more.

A PRAYER FOR A PURE HEART
AND HEAVENLY WISDOM

Strengthen me, O Lord God, with the grace of Your Holy Spirit.[3] Give me inward strength and power[4] and empty my heart of all profitless concern and anxiety.[5] Let me never be drawn away from You through desire for anything else, whether noble or unworthy, but help me to realize that all things are transitory, including myself. Nothing in this world is lasting and everything in this life is futile and disturbing to the spirit.[6] It is the wise who know these truths. O Lord, give me heavenly wisdom, so that above all else I may learn to search for and discover You; to know and love You; and to see all things as they really are and as You in Your wisdom have arranged them. May I wisely avoid those who flatter me, and deal gently with those who oppose me. Pure wisdom cannot be moved by every verbose argument[7] and pays no regard to the cunning flatteries of evil people. Only so shall we move forward steadily on the road which we have begun to tread.

TWENTY-EIGHT

Against slanderous talk

CHRIST: My child, do not mind if others think ill or say unpleasant things about you. Think of yourself as much worse than they imagine, and regard no one as weaker than yourself. If your inner life is strong, you will not pay much attention to trivial words. When attacked by evil, the wise stay silent. They turn their hearts to Me and are untroubled by the judgements of others.

Do not let your peace depend on what other people say about you. Whether they speak well or ill of you makes no difference to what you really are. True peace and joy is to be found in Me alone. Those who are neither anxious to please, nor afraid to displease, enjoy real peace. All unrest of heart and distraction of mind comes from distracted feelings and groundless fears.

TWENTY-NINE

How we should call on God in all trouble

DISCIPLE: Praised be Your holy name for ever, O Lord.[1] I know that temptation and trouble come upon me by Your holy will. I cannot escape it, but have to come to You for help, so that all may be turned to good. Lord, I am tormented and uneasy in my mind and my present troubles weigh heavily upon me. Most loving Father, what can I say? I am in a tight corner. 'Save me from this hour.'[2] Yet it is for Your glory that I have been brought to this moment and so that I can learn that only You can save me from the depths of my humiliation. O Lord, save me by Your goodness.[3] For what can I do, helpless as I am, and where can I go without Your help? Lord, grant me patience even in this trial. However hard pressed I may be, help me and I shall fear nothing.

In my trouble, my prayer now will be, 'Your will be done.'[4] I have totally deserved this trouble and must put up with it. Let me bear it with patience until the storm is past and better days return. I know that Your almighty hard can remove even this trial from me and weaken the violence, so that I am not totally crushed by it. My God and my Mercy, You have done this for me many times in the past. O Most High God, the harder it is for me, the easier it is for You to change my ways.[5]

THIRTY

*On asking for God's help and confidence in
His saving grace*

CHRIST: My child, I am the Lord who gives help in times of
trouble.[1] Come to Me when the battle is hard for you.[2] The
greatest obstacle you have to receiving My heavenly comfort is
your reluctance to pray. For when you ought urgently to seek
Me, you first turn to many other comforts, and hope to save
yourself by worldly means. It is only when these things have
failed that you remember that I am the Saviour of all who put
their trust in Me.[3] Apart from Me, there can be no help,[4] no
good advice and no lasting cure. But now, after the storm, with
a renewed spirit, gather fresh strength and light through My
mercies.[5] For I am near at hand and will restore all things, not
only completely, but generously overflowing with extra graces.

Is anything too hard for Me?[6] Am I like someone who lets
you down? Where is your faith? Stand firm and persevere. Be
confident and courageous and help will arrive for you in due
time. Wait patiently for Me and I will come and heal you
Myself. Temptation is to test you – there is no reason for fear
or anxiety. If you worry about the future, sorrow upon sorrow
will be the result. Each day has troubles enough of its own.[7] It
is silly and useless to be either anxious or pleased about the
future, for whatever you anticipate may never happen.

The human mind is prone to delusions, but it is a sign of
spiritual weakness to be deceived by the propositions of the
Devil. Satan does not care whether it is through truth or falsehood that he mocks and deceives you, or whether he obtains
your downfall through the love of the present or fear of the

future. So set your troubled heart at rest and banish your fears.[8] Trust in Me and put your whole confidence in My mercy.[9] It is when you think that I am far away from you that I am nearest to you. And when the battle looks to be lost, then the reward for all your work is often close at hand. When things turn out contrary to your plans that does not mean that all is lost. So do not allow your temporary feelings to obscure your judgement. Do not give in to depression, as if all hope of recovery were lost.

Do not imagine that you are totally forsaken if, for some time, I have allowed some trial to test you or withdrawn the consolation which you desire, for this is the way to the Kingdom of Heaven. Be assured that it is better for you and for all My servants to struggle against difficulties than to have everything that you want. I know your secret thoughts and it is necessary for your salvation that you should sometimes be deprived of spiritual joys, lest you become conceited in your smug state and complacently imagine that you are better than you are. What I have given, I can take away and give back when I choose.

When I grant great comfort, it is still Mine. When I take it away I am not taking anything that is yours, for every good gift and every perfect gift is Mine alone.[10] If I send you trouble and affliction, do not be indignant or downhearted; for I can quickly help you and turn all your sorrow into joy.[11] Nevertheless, I keep My own counsel, and in all My dealings with you give Me due praise.

If you are wise and have right judgement, you will never despair or be discouraged. On the contrary, if I scourge you with trouble and do not spare you, be glad and grateful, and regard it as a cause for joy.[12] 'As the Father has loved Me, so I have loved you',[13] were My words to My beloved disciples, whom I did not send out to enjoy the pleasures of the world, but to fight hard battles; not to win honours, but contempt; not to be idle, but to work hard; not to rest, but to bring forth much fruit with patience.[14] My child, remember these words.

THIRTY-ONE

On neglecting all creatures to find the Creator

DISCIPLE: Lord, if I am to reach the state where no creature can impede my progress, I am in very great need of Your most abundant grace. For as long as anything restrains me, I cannot freely come to You. Someone who desired to fly to You freely said, 'O that I had wings like a dove! I would fly away and be at rest.'[1] And who is more perfectly at rest than the person who is single-minded?[2] The most free person is one who desires nothing from the earth. Captivated by the spirit, we can rise above all created things and, leaving self behind, we can see clearly that nothing in creation compares to the Creator. But we cannot freely turn to the things of God unless we are freed from dependence on creatures. That is why there are so few contemplatives, for there are few who can release themselves totally from passing things.

A soul needs great grace to be lifted up and carried beyond itself. And unless a soul is raised up, set free from all attachment to earthly things and wholly united to God, neither knowledge nor possessions are of much value. As long as anything is esteemed as more precious than the one, infinite and eternal Good we remain mean, earthbound spirits. For whatever is not God is nothing, and is counted as nothing. There is a great difference between the wisdom of a devout person enlightened by God and the knowledge of a learned and studious scholar. The learning influenced by divine grace is far more noble than that painfully acquired by human endeavour.

Many people desire the grace of contemplation, but few take the trouble to practise what is essential to it. It is a great obstacle if we rely on external signs and the experience of the senses and pay little regard to the perfecting of self-discipline. I hardly know what it is, what spirit moves us, or what our purpose may be when we, who wish to be considered spiritual, take so much trouble and are so concerned with trivial daily affairs, and so seldom give our full and earnest attention to our interior life.

It is sad that, after a short meditation, we break off and take no strict examination of our lives. We do not reflect on where our affections really lie, nor are we grieved at the sinfulness of our whole life. Yet it was because of human wickedness that the Flood came upon the earth.[3] When our interior desires are corrupted, the actions which spring from them are also defiled. And this is a sign of our lack of interior strength, for it is from a pure heart alone that the fruits of a holy life[4] emerge.

A person's achievements are often discussed, but rarely the principles on which such a life is based. We enquire whether someone is brave, handsome, rich, clever, a skilled writer, a fine singer or hard worker. But we seldom consider whether someone is humble-minded, patient and gentle, devout and spiritual. Nature looks at our outward characteristics. Grace considers our inner disposition. While Nature is often misled, Grace trusts in God and cannot be deceived.

THIRTY-TWO

On self-denial and giving up our own desires

CHRIST: My child, the only way to perfect liberty is total self-denial. Those who are obsessed by self-interest and self-love are slaves of their own desires.[1] They are greedy, inquisitive and discontented. They indulge themselves in pleasures, but never in the service of Jesus Christ. Their whole interest lies in passing affairs. But everything that is not of God will perish totally. Keep this simple advice for perfection: 'Leave all and you shall find all.' Renounce desire and you will find peace. Give this proper thought and, when you have to put it into practice, you will understand all things.

DISCIPLE: Lord, this is not the work of a single day, and no easy matter. These few words contain the whole path of spiritual perfection.

CHRIST: My child, do not be discouraged or diverted from your purpose of learning this way of perfection. Rather, let it spur you on to higher things and, at least, to set your heart on them. If only you would do this, and attain that state where you stop being a lover of self, and stand ready to do My will and his whom I have appointed as your father, you would greatly please Me.[2] Then your whole life would be filled with joy and peace. You still have many things to renounce, and unless you surrender them to Me without reserve, you cannot obtain what you ask of Me. I advise you to buy from Me gold, refined in the fire, so that you may be rich[3] in that heavenly wisdom which rejects all worthless things. Despise the wisdom of the world, and every temptation to please yourself or others.

I have said, exchange what others consider desirable and honourable for that which they hold in low esteem. For true divine wisdom, having no exalted opinion of itself,[4] seeks no recognition from the world. It is almost disregarded by others and seems to them to be useless and of no importance. Many pay lip service, but it does not affect any part of their lives. Yet this is the precious pearl that remains hidden from many.[5]

THIRTY-THREE

*On a wayward heart and directing
all we do to God*

CHRIST: My child, do not trust your emotions, for they are changeable and wayward. In all your life you are subject to change, even against your own inclinations.[1] At one time you are cheerful, at another sad; now peaceful, now troubled; now full of devotion, now wholly lacking in it; now zealous, now lazy; now serious, now happy. But wise people who are well versed in spiritual matters stand above these changing emotions. They pay little attention to passing feelings and whims, but direct all intellectual powers towards a right and true end. So, having fixed their gaze and kept their intention constantly on Me, they can remain single-minded and unshaken in all situations.

The more single-minded a person is,[2] the more steadily they will pass through all the storms of life. But for many people this one purpose becomes obscured, for they easily pay attention to any pleasant thing which comes their way. It is very rare to find anyone who is totally free from the sin of self-interest. So the Jews once came out to Martha and Mary at Bethany, not only for Jesus' sake but to see Lazarus.[3] So make your intention pure, single and upright so that it may be directed to Me alone without any obstacles.

THIRTY-FOUR

God, above all things and in everything,
is the delight of those who love Him

DISCIPLE: My God and my All![1] What more can I possess?

What greater joy can I desire? Words of sweetness and joy to all who love the Word better than the world and its riches! My God and my All! To the wise these words will be sufficient. Those who love You will enjoy repeating them again and again.[2] When You are present, all is joy. When You are absent, all is gloom. You bring rest to the heart, true peace and true happiness. You lead us to think well of all and to praise You in all, for nothing can give us lasting joy without You, but if it is to be enjoyable and to our taste it must contain Your grace and be seasoned with Your wisdom.

Whoever knows Your joys will find joy in all things; but whoever knows nothing of Your joys will find no joy in anything. Those who are worldly wise and sensually minded lack Your wisdom, for a great deal of vanity lurks in the world, and death in the flesh.[3] The truly wise are those who follow You by despising worldly things and suppressing their bodily desires; they abandon illusion for truth, they forsake the flesh for the spirit. They rejoice in God alone, and whatever good they discover in creatures they ascribe wholly to the glory of their Maker. But what a great difference there is between the enjoyment of the Creator and the enjoyment of His creation; between eternal things and temporal things, between uncreated light and created light!

A PRAYER FOR LIGHT

O Light everlasting, surpassing all created light![4] Pour out from heaven the glorious rays of Your light; pierce the very depths of my heart! Purify, cheer, enlighten and enthuse the powers of my spirit, so that it may cling to You with unspeakable joy. Oh when will that blessed and longed-for time come? When will You fill me with Your presence and be All in All to me?[5] I can know no fullness of joy until You grant me this. Alas, my lower nature is still strong within me; it is not yet crucified, nor totally dead.[6] It still fights strongly against the spirit, stirs up conflicts inside me, and will not allow the kingdom of the soul to stay at peace. O Christ, ruler of the power of the sea and calmer of its raging waves,[7] come near and help me. Disperse the nations who delight in war[8] and overwhelm them through Your strength.[9] Reveal Your mighty power, I pray. Show Yourself glorious in might. O Lord my God, my only hope and refuge[10] lies in You.

THIRTY-FIVE

How there is no security from temptation in this life

CHRIST: My child, there is no security from temptation in this life and, as long as you live, you will need a spiritual armoury. Your road lies through enemies and you are liable to attack on every side. Unless you carry the shield of patience[1] you will not long remain without wounds. And unless you fix your heart on Me, with a firm resolve to suffer gladly for My sake, you will not endure the heat of battle, nor win the crown of the Saints. Tolerate everything bravely and strike boldly at your enemies, for the bread of heaven is the reward of the victor[2] and the lazy are left in unspeakable misery.

How will you gain eternal rest if you look for leisure in this life? Do not choose to have rest, but patient endurance. Do not seek true pleasure on earth but in heaven; not in people nor in any other creature but in God alone. Tolerate everything for the love of God – work, sorrow, temptation, provocation, anxiety, necessity, weakness, injury and insult; abuse, humiliation, disgrace, contradiction and contempt. All these things encourage your growth in virtue, for they test the untried servant of Christ and form the jewels of His heavenly crown. I will give an eternal reward for your brief toil and endless glory for your transitory trouble.

Do you think that you can always have spiritual benefits whenever you want? My Saints did not; they had many troubles, countless trials and great desolation of the soul. But they patiently endured all these things and trusted in God rather than themselves. They knew that 'the sufferings of this present time are not worth comparing with the glory about to be revealed to us.'[3] Do you want to enjoy now what many others have won only after much sorrow and struggle? Wait for the Lord; fight bravely and with great courage.[4] Do not despair, do not desert your task, but steadfastly devote yourself, body and soul, to the glory of God. I will be with you in all your troubles[5] and will give You a rich reward.[6]

THIRTY-SIX

Against vain human judgements

CHRIST: My child, trust in God with all your heart. If your conscience affirms your devotion and innocence, you need not fear people's judgement. It is a good and holy thing to suffer in this way, and it will not be a burden to the humble heart that trusts in God rather than itself. Do not pay any attention to people who talk too much. Moreover, it is quite impossible to please everyone. Although St Paul tried to be pleasing to everyone in the Lord[1] and become all things to all people, he cared very little about what they thought of him.[2] He did whatever lay in his power to bring instruction and salvation to others, but even he could not escape being misjudged and despised by others. Accordingly he entrusted himself wholly to God, who knows all things, and he preferred the shield of patience and humility to the unjust accusations, empty lies and cheap boasts of his detractors. Nevertheless, he sometimes replied to them lest his silence should give offence to the weak.[3]

Why should you fear humans, who must die?[4] They are here today and tomorrow gone for ever. If you fear God, you will never fear anyone else. What harm can come from the words and actions that people can do to you? They injure themselves rather than you, whoever they are; they never escape the judgement of God. Keep God always before you and do not engage in angry controversies. Even if you seem to suffer defeat and undeserved disgrace at present, do not complain or through impatience[5] reduce your due reward. Instead, lift your eyes to Me in heaven. I have power to deliver you from all shame and wrong and reward everyone according to their merits.[6]

THIRTY-SEVEN

*How total self-surrender brings us
freedom of heart*

CHRIST: My child, deny yourself and you will find Me.[1] Have
no self-interest or choice of your own and you will always be
the winner. As soon as you surrender yourself unconditionally
into My hands, I will give you even richer graces.

DISCIPLE: Lord, how often shall I surrender myself and in
what way reject myself?

CHRIST: Always and at all times, in little things as well as
great ones. I make no exception, for I want to own you, totally
divested of yourself. Otherwise, unless you are totally stripped
of self-will, how can you be Mine and I belong to you? The
sooner you do this, the better it will be with you. The more
completely and sincerely you do it, the better you will please
Me and the greater will be your gain.

Some surrender themselves, but with some reservations.
They do not put their whole trust in God, and so are concerned
to provide for themselves. Others offer everything at first, but
later are overcome by temptation and return to their former
state. These make little progress in virtue and they will never
gain the true freedom of a pure heart, nor enjoy the favour of
My friendship,[2] unless they make a complete surrender and a
daily offering of themselves to Me. Without this no creative
union with Me will exist or endure.

I have frequently said to you, and now I say it once more:
renounce yourself, surrender yourself and you will enjoy great
inner peace. Give all for all, look for nothing, ask for nothing
in return; stay simply and trustingly in Me and you will possess
Me. Then you will be free in heart, and no darkness will oppress

your soul. Strive for this, pray for this, desire this one thing, so that you may be stripped clean of all selfishness and follow Jesus in total self-abandonment, dying to self, so that you may live in Me for ever. Then all vain fantasies will be put to flight, and all evil disorders and empty fears will vanish. Then all fear and dread will go away and all disturbed love will die in you.

THIRTY-EIGHT

*On a good rule of life and turning to
God in danger*

CHRIST: My child, take great care in all you do, in every place and in public dealings, so that you stay inwardly free and your own ruler. Make sure that you control your circumstances; do not let them control you. Only in this way can you rule and control your actions, not be their slave or servant: a free person and a true Christian and sharing the fortune and liberty of God's children.[1] They stand above temporal things, and look at the eternal, seeing both the earthly and heavenly in their true perspective. The things of this world do not control the children of God. On the contrary, they draw them into their service and they take these things to use in God's service, and in the ways ordained by God, and designed by the heavenly Architect. He has left nothing in His creation without its proper place.

Stand firm at all times. Do not judge by outward appearances or reports as others do, but in each situation enter into the Tabernacle (as Moses did)[2] and ask the Lord's guidance. Sometimes you will receive God's answer and come back informed on many matters, both present and future. For Moses always went to the Tabernacle to gain an answer to his doubts and questions. He took refuge in prayer to support him among the world's dangers and wickedness. So you must take refuge in the depths of your heart and pray ardently for God's help. We read that Joshua and the children of Israel were deceived by the Gibeonites[3] because they had not asked counsel of God first. So, in being ready to believe their statements, they were misled by false piety.

THIRTY-NINE

How we should not be over-anxious

CHRIST: My child, always commit your concerns to Me, and I will bring them to a fruitful end in due course. Wait until I order it, and you will find it to your advantage.

DISCIPLE: Lord, I willingly commit everything into Your hands, for my own judgement is of little value. I would like to be less concerned about the future, and more willing totally to submit myself to Your good pleasure.

CHRIST: My child, people often work endlessly to gain the things they desire but, when they gain them, they begin to change their minds. For their affections are not lasting but tend to move from one thing to another. Therefore it is no small thing if you can renounce self even in little things. True spiritual progress depends on self-denial, and those who renounce self are completely free and safe. But the Old Enemy,[1] the Adversary of everything good, never ceases to tempt. Night and day he lies in ambush, hoping to trap the unwary into the snares of his deceit. 'Stay awake and pray that you may not come into the time of trial.'[2]

FORTY

How we have no personal goodness
of which to boast

DISCIPLE: Lord, 'what are human beings that You are mindful of them, mortals that You care for them?'[1] What have we done to deserve Your grace? Lord, I have no reason to complain if You abandon me; and if Your will is contrary to my desires, I have no right to appeal against it. But I might rightly think and say, 'Lord, I am nothing and I can do nothing. I have no good in me, but am imperfect in every respect and am always prone to nothing. I become weak and utterly helpless unless You guide my soul and give me strength.'

O Lord, You remain always Yourself,[2] abiding in eternity, good, just and holy, ruling all things in goodness, justice, holiness and ordering them by wisdom. But I am always more ready to slip back, rather than go forward. I never remain the same, for seven times have passed over for me.[3] But when You deign to stretch out Your hand to help me, my state is soon changed for the better. For You alone, without human aid, can help and strengthen me, so that I may no longer be unreliable, but turn my heart to You alone, and be at peace. No human being can comfort me, and if only I could totally renounce all human support – whether to increase my devotion or because my desires compel me to seek You – then I could properly trust entirely to Your grace and rejoice in the gift of Your renewed consolation.

When things go well for me, I offer thanks to You, from whom everything proceeds. Before You I am empty nothingness, a weak and unstable person. I have nothing of which to boast, nothing which deserves any recognition. Can nothing boast of its nothingness? That would be the height of vanity. False conceit is like an evil disease, and the most monstrous of vanities, for it leads a person away from proper glory and robs them of divine grace. For as long as someone is filled with complacency, You are displeased. While there is a desire for popularity and praise, true virtue is removed. True glory and holy joy are to be found in giving glory, not to oneself but to You; rejoicing not in one's own strength but in Your name; taking no pleasure in any created thing unless it be for Your sake, blessed be Your holy name, not mine.

I will praise Your name, but not my own; I will value Your actions, not my own; I will bless Your holy name; I have no desire for human praise. You alone are my glory. You alone are the joy of my heart. I will offer You praise and glory at every hour of the day; but as for me, I will glory in nothing, unless it is my own weakness.[4] Let the Jews seek such glory as people give to each other.[5] I will seek the glory that only God can give. For all human glory, all this world's honours, all earthly titles, compared with Your eternal glory, are just futility and foolishness.

O blessed Trinity, my God, my Truth, my Mercy, to You alone let all things ascribe all praise, honour, power and glory throughout eternity.[6]

FORTY-ONE

On contempt for worldly honours

CHRIST: My child, if you see others given honours and promotion while you are overlooked and humiliated, do not be discouraged. Lift your heart to Me in heaven and human contempt will not trouble you.

DISCIPLE: Lord, we are blind and are easily deceived through self-esteem. If I carefully examine my life, I find that no creature has ever done me wrong, and I have no right to complain. But, because I have so often grievously sinned against You, it is right that everyone opposes me. I justly deserve shame and contempt; but to You, O Lord, be praise, honour and glory. Unless I am ready, willing and pleased to be despised and rejected by everyone and to be regarded as of no consequence, I cannot gain inward peace and stability, nor can I become spiritually enlightened and totally united to You.

FORTY-TWO

Peace of mind does not depend on people

CHRIST: My child, if your peace depends on someone because of your affection or friendship, you will always be unsettled and become unreliable. But, if you turn to the living and eternal truth, the departure or death of your friend will not distress you. Your love for a friend must rest in Me, and those who are dear to you in this life must be loved only for My sake. No good and lasting friendship can exist without Me, and unless I bless it and love it, it cannot be pure and true. You should be so mortified in your affection towards loved ones that, for your part, you would forego all human companionship. As people withdraw further from the consolations of this world, they draw nearer to God. The deeper they descend into themselves and the lower they regard themselves, the higher they ascend towards God.

Those who attribute any good to themselves obstruct the coming of God's grace; for the grace of the Holy Spirit always seeks a humble heart. If you would perfectly overcome self and set yourself free from love of creatures, I would come to you with all My grace.[1] While your interest is in creatures the vision of the Creator is hidden from you. So, for the love of the Creator, learn to overcome self in everything and you will come to the knowledge of God. But as long as anything, however small, occupies too much of your love and attention, it injures the soul and holds you back from attaining the highest Good.

FORTY-THREE

Against useless and worldly learning

CHRIST: My child, do not allow fine phrases and subtle sayings to entrance you. 'For the Kingdom of God depends not on talk but on power.'[1] Pay attention to My words, for they inspire the heart and enlighten the understanding, foster contrition and bring all comfort. Never study in order to appear wise and learned; rather, study to overcome your besetting sins, for this will profit you more than the grasp of complicated problems.

When you have read and mastered many subjects always return to this basic truth: that I am He who teaches all knowledge[2] and give to My children a better understanding than others can offer. Those whom I teach will quickly gain wisdom and move further in the life of the spirit. But those who ask others about many curiosities and care little for serving Me, will discover only sorrow. In due time Christ will come, the Teacher of teachers and Lord of Angels.[3] He will hear the lessons of all. That is, He will examine everyone's conscience. Then He will search Jerusalem with lamps; the hidden things of darkness will be brought to light[4] and the language of argument will cease.

I am God, who enables the humble-minded to understand more of the ways of everlasting truth in a single moment than in ten years' study at university. I teach in silence, without the uproar of controversy, without ambition for honours, without clash of opinions. I teach people to despise earthly things, to find this present life irksome, to seek eternal things, to resist honours, to endure injuries, to place all trust in Me, to desire nothing but Myself and fervently to love Me above all things.

There was once a man who loved Me very dearly, who learned many divine secrets and spoke eloquently of Me. He profited more by renouncing everything than by studying subtleties. For to some I speak on ordinary matters; to others on specific matters; to some I graciously reveal Myself in signs and symbols; while I reveal My mysteries to those who are enlightened.

A book is only a single voice but it is not equally valuable to all who read it. I alone am the Teacher of truth, the Searcher of the heart, the Discerner of behaviour, and I give to each person as I see fit.[5]

FORTY-FOUR

On avoiding distractions

CHRIST: My child, you are bound to be ignorant about many things, so consider yourself as dead and crucified to the whole world.[1] Moreover, you must turn a deaf ear to many things and reflect only on such things as bring peace. It is better to turn away from controversies and leave everyone with their own opinions than to bother them with confrontational arguments. As long as you remain in God's grace and keep His will in your heart, you will more easily tolerate apparent discomfort.

DISCIPLE: Lord, what a state of things we have reached! We grieve over worldly loss. We work and struggle to gain some small profit, forgetting the danger to our souls and rarely considering it. We attend to matters of little or no value and neglect those of the greatest importance. For when we devote all our energies to material affairs, we quickly become immersed in them, unless we come to our senses.

FORTY-FIVE

How we should not believe all we hear
and the danger of loose tongues

DISCIPLE: Lord, 'help me in my trouble, for human help is worthless'.[1] How often have I found no loyalty where I expected to find it! And how often have I found it where I least expected it! It is useless to put our hope in people. Salvation is to be found in You alone, O God.[2] We bless You, O Lord God, in all that happens to us.

We are weak and unstable, changeable and easily deceived. None of us can defend ourselves so fully and completely that we are never deceived or in doubt. But whoever trusts in You, Lord, and seeks You with a pure heart[3] does not easily fall. And if we come across any trouble, however great, You will quickly deliver or support us. For You never abandon those who trust in You to the end. It is very rare to find a faithful friend who stands by us in all trouble. And You, Lord, are the most faithful of all friends, and there is none like You.

How wise was that holy soul (St Agatha) who said, 'My mind is firmly established and grounded in Christ.'[4] If this were true of me I would never fear anyone and no bitter words would disturb me. We cannot foresee the future or prepare for future evils; and if things that we expect often harm us, how can an unexpected event do anything but seriously affect us? Why have I not made better provision for my miserable person, and why have I trusted in others so easily? For we are but mortal and merely weak, even if people can imagine and say that we are Angels. There is no one in whom I can trust, Lord, except You who are the Truth, and who neither deceives nor can be deceived. But everyone is deceitful,[5] weak, unstable and fallible, especially in what we say, so that we should not easily believe even what at first appears to be true.

Your wisdom warns us to beware of others,[6] since our enemies are those of our own household.[7] So we should not believe those who say 'He is here' or 'He is there'.[8] I have learned this to my own cost and I only hope that it may make me more cautious and correct my foolishness. 'Be discreet,' says a neighbour, 'and keep what I tell you to yourself.' And while I remain silent about it, imagining it to be a secret, the other person will not keep the silence imposed on me, but immediately we are both betrayed and the neighbour moves on. Protect me, O Lord, from such tales and from such indiscreet folk. Do not allow me to fall under their power, nor copy their behaviour. Make my conversation truthful and trustworthy, far removed from such deviousness. For at all costs I must avoid what I do not tolerate in others.

Being silent about others makes for peace and goodwill, not believing all that is said nor repeating what we have heard. There are very few people to whom we should open our hearts. Rather, we should always seek You, who can see into every heart. We should not allow ourselves to be carried to and fro by the windy blasts of words,[9] but rather pray that our whole life, both private and public, may be ordered in conformity to Your will.

A sure way of retaining the grace of heaven is to ignore outward appearances, and carefully to cultivate such things that encourage amendment of life and fervour of soul, rather than cultivate those qualities which seem to be popular.

Very many people have been harmed by publicity and by the superficial praise of their virtues. But grace is most powerful when preserved in silence in this transitory life, which only consists of battle and temptations.

FORTY-SIX

*On having confidence in God
while words are flying about*

CHRIST: My child, stand firm and trust in Me. What are words? Just words. They fly to and fro, but do not even hurt a stone. If you are guilty, think how you can make amends. If there is nothing on your conscience, resolve to accept things willingly for God's sake. If you are not ready to bear hard blows, it is a little thing to tolerate hard words from time to time. You take such trifles to heart because you are still worldly, and pay too much attention to the opinions of others. You do not like to be corrected for your faults, because you fear their contempt and take refuge in excuses.

If you examine yourself very carefully, you will find that your heart is still full of worldly desires and silly anxieties to please people. For when you shrink from the humiliation and reproof which your faults deserve, it is clear that you are not truly humble; neither are you dead to the world, nor is the world crucified to you.[1] Listen only to My words and you will care nothing for ten thousand words from others. Even if you were charged with every crime that could be maliciously invented, how could it harm you if you let it pass and paid absolutely no attention to it? Could such a flood of words harm a single hair of your head?[2]

But those who keep no guard over their hearts and do not regard God are easily unsettled by a word of reproof. Those who trust in Me and do not cling to their own judgement will fear no one. For I am the judge and the discerner of secrets. I understand the motives for every action. I know both those who inflict wrong and those who suffer it. It is by My will and permission that events happen, so that the thoughts of many hearts may be revealed.[3] I will judge both the guilty and the innocent, but first I wish to try them in My secret court.

What people say in evidence is often false, but My judgement is true; it will stand and will not be set aside. It is hidden from many and only revealed in its fullness to very few. But even if it may appear unjust to the foolish it is not and cannot be in error. So always come to Me for justice and put no trust in personal opinions.

A just person will not be anxious whatever God allows to happen.[4] Even if groundless accusations are brought, there is no need to worry. Nor should we be elated unduly if we are fairly acquitted by others, for everyone knows that it is I who examine both the heart and the senses and do not judge by outward appearances.[5] For what some see as commendable is often blameworthy in My sight.

DISCIPLE: O Lord God, most just Judge, strong and patient, who knows all our weakness and wickedness, be my strength and all my trust, for my conscience alone is not sufficient. You know what is unknown to me, and so, when blamed, I should have humbled myself and taken it meekly. Be gracious and pardon the occasions when I have not done this, and once again give me grace to endure more patiently. Your overflowing mercy will help me much more in obtaining pardon than my supposed innocence can satisfy my inmost conscience. For, although I may not be aware of any fault, yet this does not absolve me.[6] If You withhold Your mercy, no one living can be absolved in Your sight.[7]

FORTY-SEVEN

How all troubles must be borne for the sake of eternal life

CHRIST: My child, do not allow the work that you have undertaken for My sake to crush your spirit, nor let any hardships discourage you. Let My promise always be your strength and comfort. I can give you limitless reward. You will not work here for long, nor will you always experience sorrow. Wait for a little while, and you will see a speedy end to your troubles. The time will come when all work and trouble will cease. Everything temporal is bound to be short-lived and of little consequence.

Continue what you are doing with all your might; work faithfully in My vineyard.[1] I will be your reward.[2] Write, study, worship, be penitent, keep silence and pray. Boldly face all your troubles. Eternal life is worth all of this and greater struggles. Only the Lord knows the time when peace will come. It will not be day or night as we understand it,[3] but it will be everlasting light, endless glory, abiding peace and sure rest. Then you will not say, 'Who will rescue me from this body of death?'[4] or cry out, 'Woe is me, that I am an alien in Meshech',[5] for the power of death will be totally broken[6] and full salvation assured. No anxiety will remain but only the blessed joy in the pleasant and lovely fellowship of the Saints.

If only you could see the Saints crowned in eternal glory,[7] you would at once humble yourself in the dust and prefer to be the servant of all rather than dominate a single person. The Saints are now exalted as high as they were formerly seen as low by this world, despicable and unfit to live. You would not yearn after a pleasant time in this life, but prefer to suffer happily for

God's sake and regard it as the greatest gain to be considered of no importance by others.[8] If the things of God were your true delight and penetrated your innermost being, you would never complain. Should not all labour be endured for the sake of eternal life? It is no small matter to win or lose the Kingdom of God. Lift your eyes to heaven. See, here I am, and with Me are all My Saints, who in this world fought a great fight.[9] They are now filled with joy and consolation; they are now safe and at rest,[10] and they shall remain with Me for ever in the Kingdom of My Father.[11]

FORTY-EIGHT

On eternity and the troubles of this life

DISCIPLE: O ever-blessed palaces of the heavenly city![1] O glorious day of eternity, on which night never casts its shadows and whose perpetual light is total truth! O day of unending gladness and of everlasting and unchanging protection! How greatly I long for the dawning of that day and the end of all temporal things. This day already shines on the Saints, resplendent in eternal glory; but to us who are pilgrims on earth[2] it seems dim and distant.[3] The citizens of heaven now taste the joys of this day; but we, exiled children of Eve,[4] mourn our bitterness and tiredness. The days of this life are short and evil[5] and full of grief and pain.[6] Here we are defiled by many sins, trapped by many passions and prey to countless fears. Afflicted by many cares and distracted by many bizarre things, we are entangled in many follies. We are hedged about by many errors, worn out by many labours, weighed down by temptations, weakened by pleasures, tormented by need.

Oh, when will all these evils come to an end? When will I be set free from the unhappy slavery of sin?[7] O Lord, when will my mind be fixed on You alone?[8] When shall the fullness of Your joys be mine? When shall I enjoy true freedom, unchecked and untroubled in mind or body? When shall true peace be established? Peace which is undisturbed and secure, outward and inward peace, guaranteed in every way? Good Jesus, when shall I stand in Your presence?[9] When shall I see the glory of Your Kingdom? When will You be All in All to me?[10] When shall I dwell with You in Your Kingdom, which You have prepared from eternity for those whom You love?[11]

I am left exiled and destitute in an alien land, where there are daily wars and dreadful disasters. Give me comfort in my exile and calm my grief, for my total desire and longing is for You alone. Everything in this world that offers me comfort is very distasteful: I long for deep communion with You, but I cannot achieve it. I wish to cling to heavenly things, but worldly affairs and desires, which I cannot control, hold me down. I want my mind to rise freely above these things, but my body holds me as an unwilling captive. So I struggle unhappily with myself. I am a burden to myself, for while my spirit longs to rise to heaven, my body wants to stay below.

Oh how deep is my pain! For whenever I pray and try to contemplate heavenly things, a flood of worldly thoughts pours in upon me at once. My God, do not desert me! Do not abandon Your servant in Your anger.[12] Strike with Your lightning and scatter them; release Your arrows[13] at the Enemy, and utterly defeat all his wiles. Call back all my senses to Yourself, and help me to forget all worldly things. Help me to reject with scorn all the promptings of vice.

O everlasting Truth, come to my aid and do not allow vanity to move me. Come, O joy of heaven, and put to flight everything impure. Grant me forgiveness and in Your mercy deal with me kindly when, while praying, I think of anything but You. For I freely confess that I am usually oppressed by many distractions. Often, indeed, I do not really stay in my body but am carried off by my thoughts. Where my thoughts settle, there I am, and my thoughts are most frequently with the things I love. For whatever is either naturally pleasant or agreeable comes easily to mind.

It is for this reason that You, who are the Truth, have clearly said: 'For where your treasure is, there your heart will be also.'[14] If I love heaven, I think easily of heavenly things. If I love the world, I take pleasure in the delights of the world, and grieve in its troubles. If I love my body, my imagination concentrates often on the things of the body. If I love the spirit, I love to reflect on the things of the spirit. For whatever things I love, it is of these that I am keen to speak and listen, and I have these interests always at heart.

Lord, blessed are those who for Your sake say goodbye to

every creature and forcibly overcome natural inclinations, who have crucified the wishes of the flesh through the fervour of the spirit[15] so that they may offer single-minded prayer with a quiet conscience. Having removed all worldly things from our hearts and lives, we will be worthy to take our place among the Angelic choir.

FORTY-NINE

*On the desire for eternal life and fighting
for God's promises*

CHRIST: My child, when you understand the heavenly origin
of your desire for everlasting joy, and long to escape from the
prison of the body in order to be free to contemplate My
unchanging glory,[1] then open your heart with enthusiasm and
receive this holy inspiration. Offer heartfelt thanks for My
divine generosity, which treats you so kindly, visits you with
mercy, kindles you to ardour and powerfully supports you, so
that your own nature does not lead you to relapse into worldli-
ness. You do not receive this gift through any determination or
effort of your own, but solely by the favour and grace of heaven
and God's kindness. It is given so that you may grow in virtue
and deeper humility to prepare you for further conflicts, striving with complete devotion to hold tight to Me and serve Me
with sincere goodwill.

My child, there are many fires and the ascending flames are
always accompanied by smoke. Some people's desires are aflame
for heavenly things, while they themselves are not free from the
lust of the flesh. So when they make very earnest requests to
God, they do not act simply for His glory. Your own desires,
which you think are so urgent and serious, are often like this.
For that which is tainted by self-interest is not pure or perfect.

Do not ask for what is pleasant and convenient for yourself,
but what is acceptable to Me and promotes My glory. If you
look at things in their proper light, you will prefer and follow
My guidance rather than your own desires, whatever they are. I
know your wishes and have often heard your cries. You long for
the glorious liberty of the children of God,[2] already rejoicing in

your eternal home and the joys of the heavenly country. But the time for this has not yet come. There is still warfare, work and testing. You long to be filled with the supreme Good, but you cannot attain this blessing now. 'I am that Good, wait for Me until the coming of the Kingdom of God,' says the Lord.

You must still be tested in this life, and many trials await you. Consolation will sometimes be granted to you, but not in its totality. Be very strong and courageous,[3] both in your actions and in tolerating what is contrary to nature. It is essential for you to become God's new creation[4] and be changed into another person.[5] It is often your duty to act contrary to your own inclinations and to put aside your own wishes. Other people's interests may flourish, while your own wishes are frustrated. The words of others will be listened to, while yours will be disregarded. Others will ask and receive their requests, while you ask and receive nothing. Others will be highly commended, while you are ignored. Others will be entrusted with this or that appointment, while you are not considered fit for anything. Your nature will protest at this treatment, but it will be a great achievement if you remain silent, for in these and in similar ways the faithful servant of our Lord is tested in how far you can reject and subdue everything in yourself. There is almost nothing in which we have such a need to die to self than in seeing and suffering things that go against our wishes, especially when we are instructed to do what seems inconvenient and useless. And because, being under authority, you do not presume to resist the higher power, it seems a hardship to bow to the will of another and surrender your own opinion.

My child, consider the results of your work, its coming end and its boundless reward. It will not make you miserable but will powerfully strengthen your determination. In exchange for the surrender of your own will, you will always have your will in heaven. It is there that you will find all that you want, all that you can desire. There you will enjoy all good things without fear of loss. There your own will shall always be in accord with Mine and you will desire no selfish good but only Me. No one will oppose you there, no one will complain about you, obstruct or frustrate you. Everything you desire will be at hand

and stimulate your love and fill it to overflowing. There you will receive glory in return for the insults you have suffered here: a garment of splendour[6] instead of grief, and in return for your humble place on earth a throne in My heavenly Kingdom. Then the fruit of your obedience will appear, your acts of penance will be turned into joy and your previous humble subjection crowned with glory.

So, for the time being, acquit yourself in humility before everyone and do not mind who it is who speaks or commands. Take care that, whether it be your superiors, your inferiors or your equals who make any request or suggestion, you take it all in good part and sincerely try to fulfil their wishes. Let others seek many different things, one enjoying this, another that, and being highly commended for it. For your part, take pleasure in none of these things, but think little of yourself and only of My good pleasure and honour. Let this be your constant desire – that whether in life or in death, God may at all times be glorified in you.[7]

FIFTY

*How, at times of desolation, we should put
ourselves into God's hands*

DISCIPLE: O Lord God, our heavenly Father, be You now and
for ever blessed. As You wish, so it is done; as You do, so it is
well done. May all my joy depend on You, not on myself or on
any other thing, for I am Your servant, Lord. You alone are my
true joy: my hope, my crown, my happiness and my honour. I,
who am Your servant, possess nothing that is not Your gift and
I have no merit of my own.[1] All things are Yours, both what
You have given and what You have created. From my youth up
I have been poor and in misery,[2] and my soul is often distressed
to the point of tears. Sometimes, too, it is oppressed by the sufferings that come upon me. I long for the joys of Your peace
and I pray earnestly for the peace of Your children, who are
revived in the light of Your comfort. Grant me this peace, and
fill my heart with holy joy. Then the soul of Your servant will
be full of song and totally devoted to Your service. But when
You withdraw Yourself, as You often do, I cannot follow the
way of Your commandments.[3] Instead I fall on my knees and
beat my breast, because things are not what they used to be
when Your lamp shone on my head[4] and I was protected under
the shadow of Your wings[5] from the temptations that attack
me. Most just Father, ever to be praised, this is the hour of Your
servant's trial. Father, worthy of all love, it is right that now I
should suffer something for Your sake. O Father, ever to be
glorified, the hour has come[6] which has been destined by You
from all eternity, when for a time Your servant will seem totally
defeated, yet You allow me to feel Your presence inwardly. I
will be maligned and humiliated, a failure in the eyes of the

world, broken by suffering and sickness, so that I may rise
again with You in the light of a new dawn and come to glory in
heaven. This, most holy Father, is by Your appointment and all
is done as You have ordained.

You grant this favour to Your friends,[7] so that for love of
You they may endure every trouble which You allow to come
upon them. For nothing can happen in this world without Your
foreknowledge and consent. Lord, it is good for me that You
have humbled me, so that I may learn Your just decrees[8] and
remove all conceit and presumption from my heart. It is good
for me that I have to suffer humiliation[9] so that I may seek consolation in You rather than in anyone else. So I have learned to
stand in awe of Your unsearchable judgements, which correct
both the just and the unjust with equity and justice.

I thank You that You have not spared my wickedness, but
have punished me with bitter pain, afflicted me with sorrow
and sent me troubles of every kind. Nothing under heaven can
comfort me, only You alone, O Lord my God. For You are the
heavenly physician of souls. You both wound and heal, You
cast down and raise up again.[10] Your discipline corrects me,
and Your very scourge will heal me.[11]

Most loving Father, I place myself entirely in Your hands. I
submit to Your correction, strike me until my wayward stub-
bornness surrenders to Your will.[12] Make me Your true and
humble disciple, as You desire, so that I may serve Your good
pleasure in all things. Lord, I deliver myself and all that I am
into Your correction. For it is better to be punished in this life
than in the next. All things are within Your knowledge and
nothing in our consciences is hidden from Your eyes. You know
all things before they happen and no one needs to inform You
of all the events on this earth. You know what is needful for
my progress and how much trouble helps to scour away the
rust of my wickedness. Do to me whatever You wish, and do
not reject my sinful life, which is known to no one as fully and
clearly as it is to You.

Grant me, Lord, to know all that I should know, to love
what I should love, to value whatever most pleases You and to
reject all that is evil in Your sight. Let me not judge superficially

by what I see, nor be influenced by what I hear from ignorant people but, with clear judgement, discern between the spiritual and the material, and seek Your will and good pleasure at all times and above everything else. People's minds are often deceived in their judgements and the worldly are deceived in their concern only for material things. Is anyone made better by being highly regarded by their contemporaries? Someone flatters another, and then one deceives another. The futile deceive the futile; the blind deceive the blind; the weak deceive the weak; and the greater the flattery the deeper the shame it brings with it. For the humble St Francis says, 'What every man is in Your sight, O Lord, that is what he is, and nothing more.'[13]

FIFTY-ONE

*When we fail to reach higher ends,
we should take on humble tasks*

CHRIST: My child, you cannot always burn with zeal for virtue, nor constantly remain in deep contemplation. The weakness of sinful human nature will sometimes compel you to descend to lower things and carry the burdens of this present life with sorrow. As long as you are in your mortal body, you will be subject to weariness and sadness of heart. In this life, you will often lament the burdens of your body, which prevent you surrendering yourself totally to the life of the spirit and to divine contemplation.

When this happens, you will be wise to resort to humble external tasks, and to restore yourself by good works. Wait for My coming with unshakeable trust and accept your exile and desolation of spirit with patience until I come again and set you free from all anxiety. Then you will forget all your previous toil and will enjoy inward peace. I will open before you the fine landscape of the Scriptures so that you may begin to advance in the way of My commandments with a free heart.[1] Then you will say, 'I consider that the sufferings of this present time are not worth comparing with the glory about to be revealed to us.'[2]

FIFTY-TWO

How we deserve punishment and are not worthy of God's consolation

DISCIPLE: Lord, I am not worthy of Your consolation, nor of any spiritual experience. You deal justly with me when You leave me poor and desolate. If I wept a whole sea of tears, I would still not deserve Your comfort. I am worthy of nothing but scourging and punishment, for I have frequently and deeply offended You and have failed greatly in many ways. So, bearing all this in mind, I do not deserve the smallest consolation. Yet, most gracious and merciful God, You do not want any of Your creatures to perish. Desiring to show Your generosity and goodness to those who are the objects of Your mercy,[1] You reach down to console Your servant more than I deserve and in ways beyond our knowledge; for Your consolation is not like people's empty words.

What have I done, that You should grant me any heavenly consolation? I cannot remember any good that I have done, but have been always prone to sin and slow to make amends. This is the undeniable truth. If I pleaded in any other way, You would challenge me and no one could defend me. All I have deserved for my sins is hell and everlasting fire.[2] I confess sincerely that I am only fit to be scorned and despised. I am not fit to be counted among Your faithful servants.

Although I am pained to repeat it, for the sake of the truth I will accuse myself, so that I may better deserve Your mercy. Guilty and confused, what shall I say? I can only say, 'I have sinned, O Lord,[3] I have sinned; be merciful and forgive. Allow me time to show my sorrow before I go, never to return, to the land of gloom and deep darkness.'[4] Why do You insist that guilty and wretched sinners repent and humble themselves for their offences? It is because true penitence and humbleness of heart emerge from the hope of pardon; the troubled conscience is reconciled; the lost grace is restored and humanity is spared the anger of God.[5] Thus God and the humble penitent greet each other in a holy embrace.[6] Deep sorrow for sin is an acceptable sacrifice to You, Lord, and is more fragrant in Your sight than clouds of incense. This is the precious ointment which You once allowed to be poured on Your sacred feet.[7] For You have never despised a contrite and humble heart.[8] Here, at Your feet, is the place of refuge from the hatred of the Enemy; here is the place of amendment and cleansing from every stain of sin.

FIFTY-THREE

God's grace and worldly wisdom do not mix

CHRIST: My child, My grace is precious and cannot be mixed with worldly concerns and pleasures. So if you wish to receive it, you must remove every obstacle to grace. Find a secret place[1] and love the solitary life. Do not engage in conversation with others, but instead pour out devout prayer to God, so that you may preserve a humble mind and a clear conscience. Count the whole world as nothing, and put waiting on God before all outward things. For you cannot pay attention to Me and, at the same time, enjoy worldly things. Stay detached from friends and neighbours and apart from the world's comforts. It is for this reason that the blessed Apostle Peter asks all the faithful in Christ to be as aliens in a foreign land.[2]

Those who are not attached to worldly things will face death with confidence. But a weak soul cannot bear to be so detached from all things, nor can a worldly wise person understand the freedom of a spiritual one.[3] So when someone sincerely wishes to be spiritual, there must be a renunciation of everything, friends as well as strangers, and they must be cautious of no one more than themselves. If you can gain complete mastery of self, you will easily master everything else. Triumphing over the self is the perfect victory. For those who are able to control their passions by their reason, and whose reason is subject to Me, are masters both of themselves and of the world.

If you wish to reach the height of perfection,[4] you must make a bold start. Lay the axe to the roots,[5] cut out and destroy all excessive and secret love of self and of any personal and material advantage. From this inordinate self-love emerge all those other faults that have to be completely overcome. But as soon as this evil is mastered and subdued, great peace and lasting tranquillity will follow. However, few people endeavour completely to die to self and to rise wholly above it. Consequently they remain absorbed in themselves, and quite unable to rise above the self in spirit. Those who desire to walk with Me in true freedom must mortify all irregular and undisciplined desires and have no selfish longing after any creature.

FIFTY-FOUR

On the opposite working of Nature and Grace

CHRIST: My child, study carefully the impulses of Nature and Grace, for they are opposed to one another. They work in such a subtle manner that even spiritual, holy and enlightened people can hardly distinguish between them. In fact, all people desire what is good and, in words and deeds, pretend to some sort of goodness, so that many are deceived by their appearance of virtue.

Nature is crafty and seduces many, snaring and deceiving them, and always works for her own ends. But Grace moves in simplicity, avoiding every appearance of evil. She makes no attempt to deceive, and does all things purely for love of God, in whom she rests as her final goal.

Nature is unwilling to be mortified, checked or overcome, obedient or willingly subject. Grace mortifies herself, resists sensuality, submits to control and seeks to be overcome. She does not aim at enjoying her own liberty, but loves to be under discipline and does not wish to dominate anyone. Rather she desires to live, abide and exist always under God's rule and for His sake she is willing to submit humbly to all people.[1]

Nature works for her own interests, and calculates what profit she may gain from others. Grace does not consider what may be useful or helpful to her but only what may be for the good of many.[2] Nature is eager to receive promotion and reward. Grace faithfully ascribes all honour and glory to God.[3] Nature fears shame and contempt. Grace is glad to suffer reproach for the name of Jesus.[4] Nature loves luxury and leisure for the body. Grace cannot be idle, but cheerfully welcomes work.

Nature loves to enjoy rare and beautiful things and hates the cheap and ugly. Grace takes pleasure in simple and humble things, neither despising the rough nor refusing to wear old and tattered clothes. Nature pays attention to worldly matters, enjoys this world's wealth, grieves at any loss and is angered by any defamatory remark. Grace pays attention to eternal things, and is not attached to the temporal. The loss of possessions fails to move her, or hard words to anger her, for she stores up her treasures and joy in heaven, where none of it can be lost.[5]

Nature is greedy and grasps more readily than she gives, loving to keep things for her personal use. Grace is kind and generous, shuns private interests, is contented with little and considers that 'It is more blessed to give than to receive.'[6] Nature inclines towards creatures – to the body, which is her own, to vanities, to restlessness. Grace draws towards God and virtue. Renouncing creatures, she flees the world, loathes the lusts of the flesh, limits her travels and shuns public appearances. Nature is keen to enjoy any outward satisfaction that will gratify the senses. Grace seeks comfort only in God and seeks pleasure in the supreme Good above all visible things.

Nature does everything for her own gain and interest. She does nothing without a fee, hoping either to gain some equal or greater return for her services, or else praise and favour. Grace seeks no worldly return and asks for no reward,[7] except God alone. She desires no more of life's necessities than will help to obtain the things of eternity.

Nature takes pleasure in lots of friends and relations; she boasts of aristocracy and high birth. She makes herself agreeable to the powerful, flatters the rich, and praises those who are like her. Grace even loves her enemies,[8] takes no pride in the number of her friends, and thinks little of high birth, unless it is combined with greater virtue. She favours the poor rather than the rich, and has more in common with the honourable than with the powerful. She takes pleasure in those who are honest, not in deceivers; she constantly encourages the good to work earnestly for the greater gifts[9] and, by means of these virtues, to become like the Son of God.

Nature is quick to complain of need and hardship. Grace bears poverty with courage. Nature, struggling and striving on her own behalf, turns everything to her own interest. Grace refers all things to God, from whom they come. She attributes no good to herself. She is not arrogant and presumptuous. She does not argue and exalt her own opinions before others, but submits all her powers of mind and perception to the eternal wisdom and judgement of God.

Nature is curious to know secrets and to hear news. She loves to be seen in public, and to enjoy experiences. She desires recognition, and to do such things to win praise and admiration. Grace does not care for news or novelties, because all these things spring from ancient human corruption,[10] for there is nothing new or lasting in this world.

Grace therefore teaches us how the senses are to be disciplined and proud complacency avoided; how anything prone to excite praise and admiration should be humbly concealed; and how in all things and in all knowledge some useful fruit should be sought, together with the praise and honour of God. She wants no praise for herself or her actions, but desires that God may be blessed in His gifts, who out of pure love bestows all things.

Grace is a supernatural light and the special gift of God,[11] the token of His chosen and the pledge of salvation.[12] It lifts humanity from earthly things to love the heavenly, and from the temporal to the spiritual. So the more nature is controlled and overcome, the richer is the grace given while people are daily, by new visitations, being inwardly renewed according to the image of the Creator.[13]

FIFTY-FIVE

*On the corruption of Nature
and the power of Grace*

DISCIPLE: O Lord my God, You have created me in Your own image and likeness.[1] Grant me this great grace, so essential to my salvation, that I may conquer the lower elements of my nature[2] which pull me down into sin and hell. I can feel inside my own being the power of sin battling against the rule of my mind, leading me to being an obedient slave to all kinds of sensuality. I cannot resist these onslaughts unless Your most holy grace is poured brightly into my heart to help me.

I need Your grace in the fullest measure to suppress that nature which has always inclined to evil from my youth upwards.[3] For it fell through Adam, the first human being, and was tainted by sin, with the penalty of that fault descending upon all humanity. So the nature which You created good and upright has now become the total expression of corruption and weakness; for when it is left to itself it turns always towards evil and low things. The little strength that remains is only like a small spark, buried beneath ashes. This same natural reason, though hidden in deep darkness, still retains the power to know good and evil, and to discern truth and falsehood. But it is powerless to do what it knows to be good; neither does it enjoy the full light of truth, nor its former healthy attachments.

So, O Lord my God, it happens that while I inwardly delight in Your law[4] and know that Your commandments are good, just and holy,[5] both for the condemnation of all evil and the avoidance of sin, yet in my body I serve the law of sin[6] and obey my sensual desires rather than my reason. Hence, while I indeed do possess the will to do what is good, I find myself powerless to follow it.[7] In this way I make many good resolutions, but, through a lack of grace to help my weakness, any small obstacle leads to discouragement and failure. Also I know the way to perfection and see clearly what I ought to do; but I am weighed down by the burden of my own corruption, and progress no nearer to perfection.

Lord, how desperately I need Your grace if I am to undertake, carry out and complete any good work! Without it I can achieve nothing. In You and through the power of Your grace all things are possible.[8] O true and heavenly grace, without which our own merits are nothing, and our natural gifts of no value! Neither arts nor riches, beauty nor strength, genius nor eloquence have any value in Your eyes, Lord, unless joined to grace. For the gifts of nature are common to all people, good and bad alike, but grace or love are Your special gift to those whom You choose; those who are sealed with this grace are counted worthy of eternal life. So excellent is this grace that neither the gift of prophecy, nor the working of miracles, nor any speculations, however sublime, are of any value without it.[9] Indeed, not even faith or hope or any other virtue is acceptable to You without love and grace.

O most blessed Grace, who makes the poor in spirit rich in virtues and the richly blessed humble in heart, come down on me! Fill me with Your comfort,[10] unless my soul faints from weariness and dryness of mind. Lord, I pray that I may find favour in Your sight, for Your grace is sufficient for me[11] even if I receive none of the things which Nature desires. However often I am tempted I will fear no evil,[12] as long as Your grace remains with me.

Your grace is my strength, my advice and my help. It is more powerful than all my enemies and wiser than all the philosophers. It is the teacher of the truth, the instructor of doctrine, the light of the heart, the consoler of all afflictions. It casts out sorrow, drives away fear, encourages devotion and leads to penitence. Without grace I am nothing but a fruitless tree or a withered branch[13] fit only for destruction. So, Lord, may Your grace always lead and follow me[14] and keep me ever concentrating on good works, through Your Son Jesus Christ. Amen.

FIFTY-SIX

How we must deny ourselves and follow
Christ to the Cross

CHRIST: My child, you will be able to enter into My life in so far as you are willing to forsake yourself. And as the absence of craving for material things leads to inner peace, so does the forsaking of self unite your heart to God. I want you to learn total self-surrender, and to accept My will without any argument or complaint. Follow me,[1] for I am the Way, and the Truth and the Life.[2] Without the Way, there is no progress; without the Truth, there is no knowledge; without the Life, there is no living. I am the Way you must follow; the Truth you must believe; the Life for which you must hope. I am the indestructible Way, the impeccable Truth, the immortal Life. I am the most noble Way, the ultimate Truth, the true Life, blessed and uncreated. If you stay in My Way, you shall know the Truth, and the Truth shall set you free[3] and you shall lay hold on eternal Life.[4]

If you wish to enter into Life, keep My commandments.[5] If you wish to know the Truth, believe Me. If you wish to be perfect, sell everything.[6] If you wish to be My disciple, deny yourself.[7] If you wish to possess the blessed Life, despise this present life. If you wish to be exalted in heaven, be humble in this world. If you wish to reign with Me, carry the Cross with Me; for none except the servants of the Cross discover the Way to blessedness and true light.

DISCIPLE: Lord Jesus, just as Your short life was despised by the world, grant that I may follow You in accepting the world's contempt. For the servant is not greater than his master, nor is the pupil superior to his teacher.[8] Let Your servant be instructed in Your life, for it is the source of salvation and true holiness. Whatever I study or hear as well as this offers me neither new strength nor greater joy.

CHRIST: My child, since you know and have studied these things, blessed are you if you do them.[9] Whoever truly loves Me, knows and obeys My commands.[10] I will love him and will reveal Myself to him,[11] and he will reign with Me in the Kingdom of My Father.[12]

DISCIPLE: Lord Jesus, let it be as You have said; and may I deserve the fulfilment of Your promise. I have accepted the Cross from Your own hands; since You have laid it upon me, I have accepted it and will carry it unto death. The life of a good Religious is in fact a Cross, but it is also our guide to heaven. We have started out; we may not turn back, nor can we abandon it. So come on, my companions! Let us go forward together! Jesus will be with us. For Jesus' sake we have taken up the Cross; for Jesus' sake let us persevere. He will be our helper, who is also our leader; He has gone before us.[13] Look, our King advances in the front line, and will fight for us! Let us follow with courage; no terrors will frighten us. We must be ready to die bravely in battle[14] and never blemish our glory[15] by deserting the Cross.

FIFTY-SEVEN

How we should not despair if we fall into occasional faults

CHRIST: My child, it is more pleasing to Me if you have patience and humility in adversity, rather than great devotion and comfort at easier moments. Why are you so distressed when you are criticized in some small matter? Even if it had been a much more serious matter, that is no reason for you to be disturbed. Let it pass. It is not your first mistake, or anything new; nor, if you live long, will it be your last. You are brave enough when you encounter no opposition. You can give good advice and encouragement to others, but when trouble knocks unexpectedly on your own door, your strength and judgement fail you. Remember the great weakness which you often experience in little troubles; yet these things happen for your own good.

Banish discouragement from your heart as best as you can, and if trouble comes, never let it depress or hinder you for long. At the least, if you cannot bear it cheerfully, tolerate it bravely. Even if you are reluctant to bear it and feel angry, control yourself and do not allow rash words to emerge from you; you may harm Christ's little ones. The violence of your feelings will soon subside and grace will return to heal your inner pain. 'As I live,' says the Lord,[1] 'I am ready to help and comfort you more than ever, if you trust Me and call on Me with devotion.'

Be of good heart[2] and prepare yourself to endure greater trials. All is not lost, however often you feel tempted or deeply troubled. You are not God, after all, just human, not even an Angel. How can you expect to remain in a constant state of virtue, when this was not even possible for an Angel of heaven,[3] nor for the first person in the Garden? I am He who grants healing and safety to those in distress,[4] and I lift up to My divinity those who acknowledge their weakness.

DISCIPLE: Lord, Your words are blessed! They are sweeter to my mouth than honey and the honeycomb.[5] What would I do in such trials and troubles as these, if You did not sustain me with Your holy words? As long as I finally come to the haven of salvation, what does the nature or size of my sufferings matter? Grant me a holy death and a joyful passing out of this world. Remember me, O my God, and lead me in the right way to Your Kingdom.[6]

FIFTY-EIGHT

How we may not search into the
mysterious judgements of God

CHRIST: My child, avoid controversies above your understanding and the unfathomable judgements of God. Do not argue why this person is forsaken and another is given great gifts; or why one is grievously afflicted while another is richly rewarded. Such things are above human understanding, and neither reasoning nor debate is fit to explain the judgements of God. So when the Enemy puts these issues into your mind, or when inquisitive people ask about them, answer with the Prophet, 'You are righteous, O Lord, and Your judgements are right.'[1] My judgements are to be respected, not debated, because they are beyond the comprehension of the human mind.[2]

Do not argue over the merits of the Saints, which is the holiest, or which the greater in the Kingdom of Heaven. This often leads to discord and unprofitable disputes,[3] feeding pride and empty boasting, which at every turn lead to envy and dissension, while one seriously seeks to praise this Saint and another that. Now, this desire to know and explore such matters is of no benefit and is displeasing to the Saints themselves, 'for God is a God not of disorder but of peace',[4] and My peace is founded on humility, not self-promotion.

Some, in their ardent enthusiasm, profess a greater devotion to one Saint than to another; but this devotion is of human origin, not divine. I am He who made all the Saints; I gave them grace; I endowed them with glory. I know the merits of each; I went before them with My blessings.[5] I foreknew My loved ones before time began.[6] I chose them out of the world;[7] they did not first choose Me. I called them by grace;[8] I drew them by mercy. I was their guide in many temptations; I poured out on them wonderful consolations. I gave them perseverance and crowned their patience.

I know them, the first and the last, and enfold them all in My boundless love. I am to be praised in all My Saints. I am to be blessed above all things, and to be honoured in each of those whom I have predestined and raised to such glory through no previous virtues of their own. Anyone, therefore, who disparages one of the least[9] of My Saints, in no way adds to the glory of a greater by so doing, for small and great alike are My creation.[10] And anyone who speaks lightly of any of the Saints, speaks lightly both of Myself and of all the company of heaven. All are one in the bonds of love; their thoughts and aspirations are one and all love each other in unity.[11]

But above all of this, they love Me more than themselves and their own virtues. Taken up out of themselves and carried beyond the love of self, they are totally involved in loving Me, in whom they rest in peace and joy. Nothing can distract or dismay them, for they are full of the eternal truth and burn with the fire of unquenchable love. So let the wicked and worldly refrain from disputes about the standing of the Saints, for they care for nothing except their own gratification. In their own interest, they exaggerate or trivialize facts and pay no regard to the eternal truth. In the case of many, it is through ignorance, especially those who have little understanding and are seldom capable of loving anyone with a pure and spiritual love. Such people are strongly attracted to one person or another by natural affection and human friendship. As they behave towards people on earth, so they imagine that they can react to the Saints in heaven. But the thoughts of imperfect people are greatly below those given to spiritual perception through the revelations of God.

So beware, My child, of being very curious about matters beyond your knowledge. Let your aim be to be counted even among the least in the Kingdom of God. Even if you could know who is the holiest and greatest in the Kingdom of Heaven, what use would that knowledge be, unless it leads you to humble yourself before Me and rise up to praise My name with greater devotion? It is far more acceptable to God that you consider the enormity of your own sins, the smallness of your virtue and how far you are from the perfection of the Saints, than that you should argue about who is the greater or lesser among them. It is better to pray to the Saints with devout prayer and sorrow, and to implore their glorious prayers, than to search into their secrets with pointless curiosity.

The Saints enjoy good and perfect contentment. Oh, if only people could be content and control their empty talk! The Saints do not boast of their own virtues; they attribute no goodness to themselves, but only to Me, for I gave them everything through My endless love. They are filled with such a deep love for God and with such an overwhelming joy that nothing is wanting to their glory, nor can anything be lacking in their happiness. The higher they stand in glory, the more humble the Saints are in themselves and the closer they are to Me and more loved. So you have the biblical words, they 'fall before the One who is seated on the throne and worship the One who lives for ever and ever'.[12]

Many ask, 'Who is the greatest in the Kingdom of Heaven?'[13] not knowing whether they themselves will ever be counted even the least in it. It is a great thing to be even the least in heaven, where all are great, for all shall be called the children of God[14] and will really be so. The least shall be equal to a thousand ordinary people, but the sinners, for all their hundred years, will die.[15] When the disciples asked who should be the greatest in the Kingdom of Heaven, they received the reply: 'Unless you change and become like children, you will never enter the Kingdom of Heaven. Whoever becomes humble like this child is the greatest in the Kingdom of Heaven.'[16]

Woe to those who are too proud willingly to humble themselves like little children, for the humble gates of heaven will not open to let them in. Woe also to the rich, who enjoy their pleasures in this life,[17] for while the poor enter into the Kingdom of God, they shall stand weeping outside. Be glad, you humble people! Leap for joy, O you poor! If you will but live in the Truth, the Kingdom of God is yours.[18]

FIFTY-NINE

That we should hope and trust in God alone

DISCIPLE: Lord, in this life in what can I put my trust? And what is my greatest comfort on earth? Is it not only You, O Lord my God, whose mercy is endless? Have I ever prospered without You? And did I suffer badly when You were at hand? I would prefer to be poor for Your sake than rich without You. I would choose to be a vagrant on the face of the earth with You rather than possess heaven without You. For where You are, there is heaven, and where You are not, there is death and hell. You are my only desire; I cry, pray and sigh for You. I cannot put my trust in any mortals to give me the help sufficient for my needs, but only in You alone, O my God. You are my hope,[1] my trust, my strength and most reliable in all things.

People seek their own interests,[2] but You, Lord, seek only my salvation and welfare, and turn all things to my good.[3] Even when You expose me to various temptations and hardships, You order them completely for my good, for that is Your way to test Your chosen servant by many trials. During trials of this kind my love and praise is Your due no less than when You fill my soul with heavenly comfort.

Then, O Lord God, I place my whole hope and trust in You. I put all my trouble and distress onto You. Whenever I look elsewhere, I find things weak and unstable. The number of my friends is no help; powerful allies will not be able to help; wise counsellors will not be able to give me useful answers, nor learned books give me comfort. No precious jewel can ransom me, nor can any secret or pleasant place offer refuge, unless You Yourself stand at my side to assist and help me, to strengthen, cheer, instruct and protect me.

Unless You stay with me, all things that seem to bring peace and happiness are as nothing, for they cannot offer true happiness. You alone are the End of all good things, the fullness of life, the depth of wisdom; the greatest comfort for Your servants is to trust in You above everything else. My God, Father of mercies, I look to You, I trust in You.[4] Bless and sanctify my soul with Your heavenly blessing, that it may become Your holy dwelling and the seat of Your eternal glory. Let nothing remain in the temple of Your glory to offend the sight of Your divine majesty. Of Your great goodness and abundant mercy look on me and hear the prayer of Your humble servant, an exile from home in the land of the shadow of death.[5] Guard and preserve the soul of Your servant among the many perils of corruptible life. Let Your grace go with me, and guide me in the way of peace[6] to my native land of perpetual light.

Notes

PART ONE: THE CHAPTERS OF BOOK ONE

ONE

1. John 8: 12
2. Mark 3: 5
3. The direct reference is to the Book of Revelation 2: 17, but it relates to the manna provided by God to the Jews in the wilderness (Exodus) and also to John 6: 46–51.
4. Romans 8: 9
5. This is a direct attack on post-Thomist theologians who argued over fine details of theology.
6. Ecclesiastes 1: 2
7. Deuteronomy 6: 13
8. Galatians 5: 16
9. Ecclesiastes 1: 8

TWO

1. Aristotle, *Metaphysics*, 1.i
2. Ecclesiasticus 19: 22
3. 1 Corinthians 13: 1–3
4. 1 Timothy 3: 9
5. Romans 11: 20

THREE

1. Numbers 12: 8
2. Jeremiah 5: 21; John 12: 40; Romans 11: 8 and Psalm 115: 4–8 in reference to idols.

3. John 1: 3
4. John 8: 25–7. The writer is referring to the Latin Vulgate translation.
5. John 14: 6
6. Jeremiah 31: 3
7. Cf. the Liturgy of St James. See the hymn 'Let all mortal flesh keep silence'.
8. Wisdom 10: 12
9. 1 Corinthians 9: 24–7
10. Matthew 7: 17–20
11. This refers to a Religious (Monastic) Community.
12. The whole section reflects Ecclesiastes 2.
13. Psalm 103: 1, 5ff. and 1 John 2: 17
14. Romans 1: 21–3
15. Philippians 2: 1–9 and 3: 8

FOUR

1. Ecclesiasticus 19: 16
2. Genesis 8: 21
3. Ecclesiasticus 14: 1
4. Tobit 4: 19
5. Ecclesiasticus 34: 9

FIVE

1. Seneca, *Letters*, XII
2. Augustine on Psalm 36
3. Psalm 117: 2; 1 Peter 2: 24–5
4. Hebrews 1: 1
5. Ecclesiasticus 6: 35
6. This refers to the early Fathers of the Church.

SEVEN

1. Psalm 118: 8–9
2. Psalm 4: 5
3. James 4: 6
4. 2 Corinthians 10: 17
5. Psalm 94: 11; John 2 : 25
6. Isaiah 55: 8

EIGHT

1. This chapter and chapters 9, 10, 11, 16, 17, 18, 19, 20 and 25 relate mainly to those under vows in Religious Communities.
2. Ecclesiasticus 8: 19

NINE

1. Cf. 1 Peter 5: 1–7

TEN

1. Matthew 26: 41
2. Ephesians 4: 29
3. James 3: 5
4. Acts 2: 42. This describes how the *devotio moderna* operated.

ELEVEN

1. Matthew 5: 8
2. Matthew 3: 10
3. 1 Corinthians 9: 27
4. Matthew 25: 23

TWELVE

1. 1 Peter 2: 11
2. John 15: 5
3. Philippians 1: 23

THIRTEEN

1. John 16: 33
2. Job 7: 1
3. 1 Peter 4: 7
4. 1 Peter 5: 8
5. Acts 14: 22
6. Ecclesiasticus 9: 11
7. James 1: 14
8. Matthew 12: 45
9. Colossians 1: 11
10. Psalm 107: 23–7
11. Ecclesiasticus 31: 26
12. Cf. Ovid, *Remedies for Love* 91, in which Ovid instructs his readers on how to extricate themselves from a love affair.

13. 1 Corinthians 10: 13
14. Judith 8: 17; 1 Peter 5: 6
15. Luke 1: 52

FOURTEEN

1. Matthew 7: 1
2. Philippians 3: 21, but this section is a reflection on Philippians 2: 3–11

FIFTEEN

1. Colossians 1: 16–19

SIXTEEN

1. Matthew 6: 13
2. Matthew 6: 9
3. Genesis 50: 20
4. Galatians 6: 2
5. Galatians 6: 5
6. 2 Corinthians 3: 5
7. Proverbs 3: 7
8. 1 Thessalonians 5: 11
9. Colossians 3: 13

SEVENTEEN

1. Philippians 3: 6
2. Revelation 2: 10
3. Stability is a great principle of the Benedictine Rule.
4. 1 Peter 2: 11; Hebrews 11: 13
5. 1 Corinthians 4: 10
6. The tonsure is the shaven head of the monk, which he is given on entering the monastery. The habit is the distinctive garment of the Order he enters.
7. Ecclesiastes 1: 18
8. Luke 22: 26–7
9. Wisdom 3: 6

EIGHTEEN

1. Hebrews 10: 32; 1 Corinthians 4: 11
2. John 12: 25

3. *Labore est orare* was the essential principle of the Religious Life. See *The Rule of St Benedict*.
4. Exodus 33: 11
5. James 4: 4

NINETEEN

1. See Psalm 139
2. Proverbs 16: 9
3. Jeremiah 10: 23
4. Ephesians 6: 11
5. This is a reference to the monastic practice of self-mortification by flagellation.
6. Romans 8: 18
7. Luke 12: 43–4; cf. Matthew 24: 47

TWENTY

1. Seneca, *Epistolae Morales* VII. The Roman writer Seneca lived at the time of Christ and died in AD 65. There are 124 of his letters on morals.
2. Mark 6: 31
3. Matthew 6: 6
4. Psalm 4: 4; Isaiah 26: 20 The author is relying on a translation in the Vulgate.
5. Ecclesiasticus 39: 1–3
6. Psalm 6: 6; Psalm 51: 7
7. 1 John 2: 17
8. Proverbs 23: 31–2
9. Ecclesiastes 1: 10
10. Ecclesiastes 2: 11
11. Psalm 121: 1; Isaiah 40: 26
12. Matthew 6: 6; Isaiah 26: 20

TWENTY-ONE

1. Proverbs 1: 7; 19: 23
2. Matthew 25: 41. This passage reflects the belief of the time about purgatory.
3. Psalm 80: 5. It is interesting that the Psalmist is called 'the Prophet' in this passage.

TWENTY-TWO

1. Luke 12: 19
2. Luke12: 15
3. Romans 7: 24; 2 Corinthians 5: 2
4. Psalm 25: 16
5. Romans 8: 21
6. Romans 8: 5
7. 1 Peter 1: 4
8. Hebrews 10: 35
9. 2 Corinthians 6: 2; cf. Ephesians 5: 14
10. Psalm 66: 11–12
11. Hebrews 10: 36
12. 2 Corinthians 5: 4; 1 Corinthians 15: 54
13. Genesis 6: 5
14. This whole passage is a reflection on Romans 7: 21–5.
15. 1 Thessalonians 5: 3

TWENTY-THREE

1. 1 Maccabees 2: 63
2. Luke 12: 37
3. Wisdom 4: 16
4. Matthew 24: 44
5. Hebrews 9: 27
6. Luke 21: 36
7. Matthew 24: 44
8. The comment on pilgrimage is an example of how the *devotio moderna* was critical of current religious practices. See J. Sumption and J. G. Davies.
9. 2 Corinthians 6: 2
10. Romans 6: 8
11. Luke 12: 20
12. Ecclesiastes 7: 2
13. Psalm 39: 7; 144: 4
14. Luke 12: 33; Galatians 6: 8
15. Luke 16: 9
16. 1 Peter 2: 11
17. Hebrews 13: 14

TWENTY-FOUR

1. Hebrews 10: 31
2. Isaiah 11: 4
3. Job 31: 14
4. Wisdom 11: 16
5. Wisdom 5: 1
6. 1 Corinthians 4: 10
7. Psalm 107: 42
8. 1 Corinthians 9: 27
9. Romans 8: 39

TWENTY-FIVE

1. 1 Peter 5: 8. These are words from the Office of Compline, which would be familiar to everyone in a Religious Community.
2. Ecclesiasticus 51: 30
3. 1 Corinthians 9: 25
4. This passage is probably autobiographical.
5. Romans 12: 2
6. 2 Timothy 3: 17
7. Psalm 37: 3
8. Matthew 7: 3
9. Psalm 133: 1
10. 1 Corinthians 2: 1–2
11. À Kempis also wrote a book of *Meditations on the Life of Jesus Christ.*
12. The Carthusians were a very strict Order founded by St Bruno in 1084. They lived in silence and in solitary cells, only joining together for worship and on special days for meals. The Cistercians wore white robes and were founded at Cîteaux in 1095. They lived a strict silent and secluded life. St Bernard of Clairvaux (1090–1153), who greatly influenced the *devotio moderna*, was the most famous monk of the Order. The community spread very rapidly in the thirteenth century. Thomas is here pointing out that the Augustinian Order, by comparison, lived an easy life.
13. 1 Thessalonians 5: 17
14. Colossians 3: 11
15. Colossians 1: 17
16. Ecclesiasticus 7: 36
17. Ecclesiasticus 19: 1

PART TWO: THE CHAPTERS OF
BOOK TWO

ONE

1. Luke 17: 21
2. Joel 2: 12
3. Matthew 11: 29
4. Romans 14: 17
5. Revelation 21: 3
6. Psalm 45: 12–14
7. This reflects the biblical Song of Songs. Cf. the early medieval French abbot Bernard of Clairvaux (1090–1153), and also à Kempis' fellow countryman John van Ruysbroeck's (1293–1381) *The Adornment of the Spiritual Marriage*.
8. John 14: 23
9. Revelation 3: 20
10. John 12: 34
11. Proverbs 3: 5; 1 Peter 5: 7. Cf. Psalms 31: 6; 118: 8; and 143: 8.
12. Hebrews 13: 14
13. Hebrews 11: 13; 1 Peter 2: 11
14. Philippians 3: 20
15. 1 Thessalonians 5: 17
16. See the prayer *Anima Christi*. This prayer, written in the early fourteenth century and commended for use at the Elevation of the Host in the Mass, would have been known by à Kempis. It contains the line, 'Within Thy wounds I feign would hide, ne'er to be parted from Thy side.' St Ignatius Loyola encouraged its use as part of the Spiritual Exercises.
17. It was St Francis (1181–1226) who received the wounds of Christ in his body, hence the use of the word 'stigmata' here.
18. Isaiah 53: 7–9
19. 2 Timothy 2: 12
20. Isaiah 54: 13
21. Romans 8: 28

TWO

1. Romans 8: 31
2. 2 Corinthians 7: 6
3. Psalm 46: 1
4. 1 Peter 5: 5

THREE

1. Galatians 6: 2; 1 Corinthians 13: 7; Ephesians 4: 2
2. Romans 12: 18; 2 Corinthians 13: 11
3. Hebrews 6: 12

FOUR

1. Matthew 5: 8
2. Romans 2: 9
3. 2 Corinthians 5: 17

FIVE

1. Matthew 7: 5
2. Matthew 16: 26
3. 1 Corinthians 4: 3
4. Mark 8: 36
5. Jeremiah 23: 24

SIX

1. 2 Corinthians 1: 12
2. 1 John 3: 21
3. Isaiah 57: 21
4. Romans 5: 3; Galatians 6: 14
5. 1 Corinthians 13: 6
6. 2 Corinthians 10: 18

SEVEN

1. John 15: 4
2. Isaiah 36: 6; Matthew 11: 7; Luke 7: 24
3. Isaiah 40: 6; Ecclesiasticus 14: 18; James 1: 10; 1 Peter 1: 24

EIGHT

1. John 11: 28. The author is making a mistake: Mary the sister of Martha is not the same person as Mary Magdalene. Mary Magdalene was a key figure in later medieval spirituality.
2. John 15: 7
3. Psalm 34: 8
4. Psalm 107: 29–30; Matthew 8: 26

NINE

1. Deuteronomy 1: 30
2. St Laurence was a deacon reputed to have been martyred in AD 258. Sixtus II was the Pope (257–8) at the time, who was also martyred. The Prefect of Rome ordered Laurence to hand over the treasures of the Church, so he collected the poor people and said to the Prefect, 'These are the treasures of the Church.' See also *The Golden Legend*.
3. Psalm 30: 6
4. Psalm 30: 7
5. Psalm 30: 8
6. Psalm 30: 10
7. Psalm 30: 11
8. Job 7: 18
9. Psalm 51: 10
10. Revelation 2: 7
11. 1 Peter 5: 8
12. Romans 8: 3–13

TEN

1. Matthew 5: 8
2. Matthew 22: 21
3. Luke 14: 10
4. John 5: 44

ELEVEN

1. Luke 14: 27; Matthew 16: 24
2. Cf. the prayer of St Ignatius Loyola (1491–1556).
3. This is a quotation from an unknown source but it is similar to passages from Proverbs.
4. Luke 10: 42
5. Luke 17: 10
6. Psalm 25: 16
7. Luke 14: 7–11

TWELVE

1. Matthew 16: 24
2. Matthew 25: 41
3. 1 Corinthians 1: 18

4. This may well be a reference to the vision of Constantine (272–337) at the Battle of Milvian Bridge when he saw a cross in the sky and heard the words 'Conquer in this sign', thus giving Christians official status.

5. Romans 8: 29

6. Matthew 16: 24, John 11: 16

7. Matthew 25: 46

8. John 19: 17

9. Romans 6: 8

10. It seems probable that this section may have influenced John Donne's poem 'The Crosse'.

11. Revelation 21: 4

12. Luke 24: 26

13. Job 14: 1

14. 2 Corinthians 4: 10

15. 1 Corinthians 9: 27

16. Ephesians 6: 10–13

17. Matthew 20: 23; 26: 42

18. Romans 8: 18

19. 2 Corinthians 12: 4

20. Acts 9: 16

21. Romans 6: 9. This whole paragraph seems to be a reflection on Romans 6.

22. Mark 8: 34

23. Acts 14: 22

PART THREE: THE CHAPTERS OF BOOK FOUR

THE VOICE OF CHRIST

1. Matthew 11: 28

2. John 6: 51

3. Luke 22: 19; 1 Corinthians 11: 24

4. John 6: 56

5. John 6: 63

ONE

1. Matthew 11: 28

2. 1 Kings 8: 27

3. Psalm 51: 4

4. Genesis 6: 9
5. 1 Peter 3: 20
6. Exodus 25: 10
7. 1 Kings 5: 7
8. Luke 7: 6
9. 1 Samuel 6: 14
10. 2 Samuel 6: 12–16
11. This reflects the views of the *devotio moderna*.
12. 1 Corinthians 1: 30

TWO

1. Psalm 36: 9
2. Luke 1: 43
3. Ephesians 2: 4
4. Psalm 23: 5
5. Psalm 78: 25
6. John 6: 35
7. Psalm 148: 5; John 1: 1–3
8. Cf. the Athanasian Creed.
9. 2 Maccabees 14: 35
10. Romans 12: 2
11. There are a few places where the author refers to 'the Mass'. 'The Eucharist' is used mainly in this translation.
12. Cf. the Nicene Creed.

THREE

1. Frequent Communion was rare at this time. Most people were simply expected to be present at the Mass for the Elevation of the Host. Frequent Communion was brought in by the Pope in the nineteenth century.
2. Psalm 46: 1
3. Psalm 86: 4
4. Luke 19: 9. The story of Zacchaeus was used in the Middle Ages as a Gospel for the dedication of a church.
5. Psalm 42: 1–2
6. Matthew 15: 32
7. Genesis 8: 21
8. The concept of the Sacrament as medicine which appears here was a common understanding of the time. Christ was seen as a pharmacist providing spiritual remedies. See B. Lang, pp. 336–7.
9. Psalm 107: 9

10. Zechariah 2: 13
11. Psalm 147: 5

FOUR

1. Psalm 21: 3
2. Psalm 106: 4
3. Psalm 34: 8
4. 1 Chronicles 29: 17
5. Isaiah 12: 3
6. The Cherubim and Seraphim in the Old Testament are winged sphinxes with human heads. They came into Hebrew religion through Canaanite influence and were seen as divine guardians at the entrance to Eden and in visions of the divine in the prophets Isaiah and Ezekiel. They also appear in the visions in the Book of Revelation.
7. Genesis 3: 19
8. Psalm 51

FIVE

1. Psalm 78: 25
2. Wisdom 12: 18
3. 1 Timothy 4: 14
4. 1 Timothy 3: 2; 2 Peter 3: 14
5. Titus 2: 7
6. Philippians 3: 20
7. Hebrews 5: 3; 7: 27
8. This passage is a description of the priest's vestment, the chasuble, worn when celebrating the Eucharist. It is derived from a Roman outer cloak and has changed in size at various times. The description here naturally refers to the pre-Reformation period. They were often highly decorated and usually had a cross on the front and the back. Different colours were used at different seasons.
9. 1 Peter 2: 21

SIX

1. Psalm 119: 105ff. There are echoes of Psalm 119 throughout the whole of the *Imitation*, probably due to the fact that the psalm was said daily in its entirety in monastic communities.

SEVEN

1. Psalm 32: 5
2. This refers to the monastic offices of prayer said through the day: Prime, Terce, None, Sext, Vespers and Compline.
3. The author makes a distinction between the offering of the Mass and the receiving of Communion because the Mass was offered daily, but people only received Communion on special days.
4. Ezekiel 18: 22; Isaiah 43: 25; Hebrews 10: 17
5. Ezekiel 33: 11; cf. 18: 23

EIGHT

1. Isaiah 53: 7; Hebrews 9: 28
2. The author does not investigate the theology of the Atonement. In the Old Testament propitiation relates to the offerings at the Mercy Seat in the Temple, done to please God. There are many theories of the Atonement but no interpretation is definitive. But all Christians regard the sacrifice of Jesus on the Cross as final and definitive.
3. Romans 12: 1
4. Philippians 4: 17
5. Ecclesiasticus 35: 7
6. Luke 14: 33

NINE

1. 1 Chronicles 29: 11
2. 1 Chronicles 29: 17
3. Psalm 51: 9; 1 John 1: 7
4. Hebrews 9: 14
5. Romans 16: 16
6. This refers to the Sacrament of Confession.
7. Psalm 25: 11
8. 1 Peter 1: 19
9. 1 Maccabees 13: 46
10. Psalm 123: 3

TEN

1. Job 1: 7
2. There were special devotions for an act of spiritual Communion when it was not possible to attend church.

3. These instructions are clearly for a priest to observe local custom and not to impose personal practices on a congregation.

ELEVEN

1. Luke 7: 38; John 12: 3. Neither passage refers to Mary Magdalene. The writer is simply following the medieval tradition about her.
2. Psalm 42: 3
3. Hebrews 1: 6
4. 2 Corinthians 5: 7
5. Song of Songs 2: 17
6. 1 Corinthians 13: 10
7. 1 Corinthians 13: 12
8. 2 Corinthians 3: 18
9. John 1: 14
10. 1 Peter 1: 25
11. Romans 1: 9
12. Hebrews 6: 12
13. Hebrews 11: 39–40
14. Psalm 119: 105
15. John 6: 35
16. 1 Samuel 21: 4
17. Hebrews 6: 19; 9: 3
18. Ephesians 4: 11
19. Luke 14: 16
20. Psalm 116: 13; cf. Psalm 23: 5
21. 1 Timothy 2: 8
22. Leviticus 19: 2

TWELVE

1. Acts 7: 49; Isaiah 66: 1
2. Mark 14: 15; Luke 22: 12
3. 1 Corinthians 5: 7
4. John 6: 56; 14: 7
5. Psalm 102: 7
6. Isaiah 38: 15
7. Luke 14: 12–14
8. Matthew 11: 28
9. Matthew 7: 7; Luke 11: 9
10. 2 Maccabees 14: 35
11. 1 Timothy 4: 14

12. Proverbs 10: 19
13. John 15: 4; Galatians 2: 20

THIRTEEN

1. Exodus 33: 11
2. John 20: 28
3. John 17: 21
4. Song of Songs 5: 10
5. Psalm 23: 6
6. Psalm 89: 46; Isaiah 45: 15
7. Proverbs 3: 33–4
8. Wisdom 16: 20; John 6: 32–5
9. Deuteronomy 4: 7
10. Psalm 116: 12
11. Cf. John 15: 4–10

FOURTEEN

1. Psalm 31: 19
2. Jeremiah 2: 13; Psalm 42: 2; Revelation 7: 17; John 4: 10
3. Luke 24: 32

FIFTEEN

1. Matthew 5: 8
2. 2 Corinthians 4: 7
3. Isaiah 60: 5
4. Psalm 119: 2

SIXTEEN

1. John 21: 17
2. John 1: 5; 2 Corinthians 4: 6
3. 1 Peter 2: 11; Ephesians 2: 19
4. 1 Corinthians 6: 17
5. Leviticus 6: 13
6. James 4: 8

SEVENTEEN

1. Luke 1: 38
2. Luke 1: 44
3. John 1: 36
4. John 3: 29

5. Song of the Three Holy Children 68
6. Psalm 150: 2
7. Revelation 7: 9

EIGHTEEN

1. Proverbs 25: 27
2. This is a reference to the writings of the early Fathers of the Church who helped to formulate Christian doctrine.
3. Psalm 119: 35
4. James 4: 17
5. Psalm 119: 130
6. Matthew 11: 25
7. This reflects St Anselm's (1033–1109) comment, 'Credo ut intelligam', which translates as 'I believe in order that I may understand.'
8. Job 5: 9
9. Psalm 135: 6
10. Isaiah 40: 28

PART FOUR: THE CHAPTERS OF
BOOK THREE

ONE

1. Psalm 85: 8
2. 1 Samuel 3: 19
3. Matthew 13: 16
4. 1 Kings 19: 12
5. Psalm 27: 1; Psalm 35: 3

TWO

1. 1 Samuel 3: 9
2. Psalm 119: 125
3. Psalm 119: 36; 78: 1
4. Deuteronomy 32: 2
5. Exodus 20: 19
6. 1 Corinthians 3: 7
7. John 6: 68

THREE

1. John 6: 63
2. Ecclesiastes 9: 17
3. Psalm 94: 12
4. Hebrews 1: 1
5. Isaiah 23: 4
6. Psalm 119: 11
7. John 12: 48
8. Genesis 18: 27
9. 2 Corinthians 12: 10
10. Job 42: 2
11. Psalm 25: 6
12. Psalm 143: 7
13. Psalm 143: 6
14. Psalm 143: 10
15. Colossians 1: 17

FOUR

1. Genesis 17: 1
2. John 8: 32
3. 1 John 3: 22
4. Tobit 3: 5
5. Psalm 119: 120
6. 2 Maccabees 7: 38
7. Isaiah 29: 13
8. Matthew 10: 20; John 16: 13

FIVE

1. 2 Corinthians 1: 3
2. Psalm 3: 3
3. Psalm 119: 111
4. Psalm 59: 16; 46: 1
5. Isaiah 40: 4
6. 1 John 4: 7
7. 1 Corinthians 13: 7. The whole chapter may be seen as a meditation on 1 Corinthians 13.
8. 2 Corinthians 11: 22–8
9. Isaiah 5: 1
10. 1 Corinthians 13: 4

SIX

1. Philippians 4: 12
2. Hebrews 12: 2
3. Matthew 4: 10
4. Jeremiah 20: 11
5. Psalm 27: 1
6. Psalm 27: 3
7. Psalm 19: 14
8. 2 Timothy 2: 3

SEVEN

1. Jeremiah 10: 23
2. Isaiah 14: 13
3. Psalm 91: 4
4. Romans 12: 16
5. James 4: 6
6. Psalm 13: 1
7. Psalm 15: 4; 131: 1–2

EIGHT

1. Genesis 18: 27
2. John 12: 25
3. Matthew 5: 45
4. Psalm 80: 19

NINE

1. Ecclesiasticus 1: 1–9
2. John 4: 14
3. John 1: 16
4. 1 Corinthians 1: 29
5. Psalm 119: 39–40
6. 1 Corinthians 13: 8
7. Luke 18: 19

TEN

1. Psalm 31: 19
2. Isaiah 57: 15
3. Luke 23: 42
4. Psalm 116: 12
5. 1 Corinthians 4: 7

6. Psalm 91: 11
7. Psalm 23: 6
8. Revelation 4: 11
9. Romans 13: 11–14
10. Matthew 7: 14

ELEVEN

1. Matthew 6: 10
2. 1 Corinthians 9: 27

TWELVE

1. Hebrews 10: 36
2. Psalm 31: 10
3. James 1: 2
4. Purgatory was seen as the place where people were purified before being fit to enter into heaven.
5. Psalm 68: 2
6. Ecclesiasticus 18: 30
7. Psalm 37: 4
8. *Confessions of St Augustine*, VIII, xi, 25
9. Revelation 12: 9

THIRTEEN

1. Genesis 3: 19
2. John 13: 14; Philippians 2: 5–10
3. Psalm 18: 42
4. Ezekiel 20: 17

FOURTEEN

1. Job 15: 15
2. Job 4: 18
3. 2 Peter 2: 4
4. Revelation 6: 13
5. Psalm 78: 25
6. Psalm 127: 1
7. Matthew 8: 25
8. Psalm 36: 6
9. 1 Corinthians 1: 29
10. Isaiah 45: 9
11. Isaiah 29: 16; 64: 8
12. Psalm 117: 2; 1 Peter 1: 25

FIFTEEN

1. James 4: 15
2. Psalm 119: 125
3. Wisdom 9: 10
4. *The Confessions of St Augustine*, V, i
5. Psalm 4: 8

SIXTEEN

1. Matthew 16: 26
2. Matthew 6: 19–21
3. St Augustine, *Sermons*, 36, 6; *City of God*, Book 11, 25.
4. Philippians 3: 20; Matthew 5: 8
5. Cf. Psalm 103: 9; Isaiah 57: 16

SEVENTEEN

1. 1 Peter 5: 7
2. Job 2: 10
3. Psalm 23: 4; Romans 8: 38
4. Psalm 77: 7
5. Revelation 3: 5

EIGHTEEN

1. John 3: 17
2. Isaiah 53: 3
3. Hebrews 12: 2
4. John 8: 12; 12: 46; Psalm 27: 1

NINETEEN

1. Hebrews 12: 4
2. Hebrews 11: 37
3. 2 Timothy 2: 3; Revelation 2: 10

TWENTY

1. Psalm 32: 5; 51: 4
2. Psalm 25: 16; 69: 14
3. Luke 11: 24–6
4. 1 John 2: 16
5. Job 30: 7
6. Psalm 34: 8

TWENTY-ONE

1. Romans 8: 19
2. Cf. St Augustine's well-known prayer, 'You have made us for Yourself and our hearts are restless until they find their rest in You.'
3. The concept of the spiritual marriage was popular at this time; see *The Adornment of the Spiritual Marriage* by à Kempis' fellow countryman, John van Ruysbroeck.
4. Psalm 55: 6
5. Psalm 34: 8
6. Revelation 22: 20
7. Psalm 27: 8
8. Psalm 119: 65; 106: 45
9. Psalm 86: 8
10. Psalm 19: 9

TWENTY-TWO

1. Psalm 119: 1; 2 Maccabees 1: 4
2. James 1: 17
3. Romans 2: 11
4. Romans 11: 36
5. John 15: 15; 1 Corinthians 1: 27
6. Psalm 45: 16
7. Acts 5: 41
8. Luke 14: 10

TWENTY-THREE

1. Matthew 26: 39
2. Matthew 10: 10
3. Luke 14: 10
4. Matthew 6: 10
5. Isaiah 45: 2
6. Psalm 122: 7
7. Matthew 8: 26
8. Psalm 89: 9
9. Psalm 43: 3
10. Genesis 1: 2
11. Genesis 27: 28; Daniel 4: 15ff.; Isaiah 18: 4
12. Genesis 2: 6

TWENTY-FOUR

1. 1 Timothy 5: 13
2. John 21: 22
3. Romans 14: 12
4. Matthew 6: 6
5. Revelation 3: 20
6. Luke 22: 46

TWENTY-FIVE

1. John 14: 27
2. Matthew 11: 29
3. Luke 11: 9
4. John 16: 13
5. Job 33: 26
6. Psalm 72: 7

TWENTY-SIX

1. Genesis 3: 17; Romans 7: 11
2. Romans 12: 21; Galatians 1: 16
3. Matthew 6: 25

TWENTY-SEVEN

1. Matthew 6: 21
2. Matthew 7: 24–7
3. Psalm 51: 12
4. Ephesians 3: 16
5. Matthew 6: 34
6. Ecclesiastes 1: 14; 2: 11
7. Ephesians 4: 14

TWENTY-NINE

1. 1 Peter 1: 3
2. John 12: 27
3. Psalm 37: 40
4. Matthew 6: 10
5. Psalm 77: 10

THIRTY

1. Nahum 1: 7
2. Matthew 11: 28

3. Psalm 17: 7
4. John 15: 5
5. Ecclesiasticus 35: 20
6. Jeremiah 32: 27
7. Matthew 6: 34
8. John 14: 27
9. Psalm 91: 2
10. James 1: 17
11. John 16: 20
12. Job 6: 10
13. John 15: 9
14. Luke 8: 15

THIRTY-ONE

1. Psalm 55: 6
2. Matthew 6: 22
3. Genesis 6: 12
4. Matthew 5: 8

THIRTY-TWO

1. 2 Timothy 3: 2
2. This could be a reference to the Superior of the community or possibly the Bishop or the Pope.
3. Revelation 3: 18
4. Romans 12: 16
5. Matthew 13: 46

THIRTY-THREE

1. Romans 8: 20
2. Matthew 6: 22
3. John 12: 9

THIRTY-FOUR

1. 1 Corinthians 15: 28; John 20: 28
2. This is a reference to the Jesus Prayer, which was used a lot in Eastern Christianity. It is the simple repetition of the phrase 'Lord Jesus Christ, Son of the Living God, have mercy on me.' See R. M. French, *The Way of a Pilgrim*.
3. Romans 8: 5
4. Psalm 27: 1; John 8: 12

5. 1 Corinthians 15: 28
6. Romans 6: 6
7. Psalm 89: 9
8. Psalm 68: 30
9. Psalm 68: 28
10. Psalm 31: 2

THIRTY-FIVE

1. Ephesians 6: 11
2. Revelation 2: 17
3. Romans 8: 18
4. Psalm 27: 14
5. Psalm 91: 15; Matthew 28: 20
6. Matthew 16: 27

THIRTY-SIX

1. 1 Corinthians 9: 22
2. 1 Corinthians 4: 3
3. Acts 26: 1; Philippians 1: 14
4. Isaiah 51: 12
5. Hebrews 12: 1
6. Romans 2: 6–7

THIRTY-SEVEN

1. Matthew 16: 24
2. Exodus 33: 11; John 15: 14–15

THIRTY-EIGHT

1. Romans 8: 21
2. Exodus 33: 8
3. Joshua 9: 22

THIRTY-NINE

1. 1 Peter 5: 8
2. Matthew 26: 41

FORTY

1. Psalm 8: 4
2. Psalm 102: 27

3. Daniel 4: 16. This verse reads: 'Let his mind be changed from that of a human, and let the mind of an animal be given to him. And let seven times pass over him.'
4. 2 Corinthians 12: 5
5. John 5: 44
6. 1 Timothy 1: 17

FORTY-TWO

1. 1 Peter 5: 5

FORTY-THREE

1. 1 Corinthians 4: 20
2. Psalm 94: 10; 119: 130
3. Colossians 3: 4
4. 1 Corinthians 4: 5
5. 1 Corinthians 12: 11

FORTY-FOUR

1. Colossians 3: 3; Galatians 6: 14

FORTY-FIVE

1. Psalm 60: 11
2. Psalm 37: 39
3. Matthew 5: 8
4. St Agatha was martyred in Sicily and her name is in the Canon of the Roman Mass. It is not clear where this saying comes from, but it is probably from the legendary Acts of her martyrdom (sixth century); see also *The Golden Legend*.
5. Romans 3: 4
6. Matthew 10: 17
7. Micah 7: 5
8. Matthew 24: 23
9. Ephesians 4: 14

FORTY-SIX

1. Galatians 6: 14
2. Luke 21: 18; Acts 27: 34
3. Luke 2: 35
4. Proverbs 12: 21
5. John 7: 24

6. 1 Corinthians 4: 4
7. Psalm 143: 2

FORTY-SEVEN

1. Matthew 20: 7
2. Genesis 15: 1
3. Revelation 22: 5
4. Romans 7: 24
5. Psalm 120: 5
6. Isaiah 25: 8
7. Wisdom 3: 1; 5: 16
8. Psalm 22: 6
9. Hebrews 10: 32; 11: 34
10. Revelation 14: 13
11. John 14: 3

FORTY-EIGHT

1. Revelation 21: 2
2. Hebrews 11: 13
3. 1 Corinthians 13: 12
4. Genesis 4: 12
5. Job 7: 6
6. Psalm 90: 10
7. Romans 7: 24
8. Psalm 71: 16
9. Psalm 51: 11
10. 1 Corinthians 15: 28; Colossians 3: 11
11. Matthew 25: 34
12. Psalm 27: 9; 71: 12
13. Psalm 144: 6
14. Matthew 6: 21
15. Galatians 5: 24

FORTY-NINE

1. John 17: 24
2. Romans 8: 21
3. Joshua 1: 7
4. Ephesians 4: 24
5. 1 Samuel 10: 6
6. Isaiah 61: 3
7. Philippians 1: 20

FIFTY

1. 1 Corinthians 4: 7
2. Psalm 88: 15
3. Psalm 119: 35
4. Job 29: 3
5. Psalm 17: 8
6. John 16: 32
7. John 11: 14
8. Psalm 119: 71
9. Psalm 69: 7
10. 1 Samuel 2: 6
11. Psalm 51: 7
12. This is a reference to the practice of using a discipline (whip) as part of penitential devotion.
13. From *The Life of St Francis* by St Bonaventure (1217–74).

FIFTY-ONE

1. Psalm 119: 32
2. Romans 8: 18

FIFTY-TWO

1. Romans 9: 23
2. Matthew 18: 8; 25: 41
3. Psalm 51: 3
4. Job 10: 21
5. Matthew 3: 7
6. Romans 16: 16
7. Luke 7: 46
8. Psalm 51: 17

FIFTY-THREE

1. Matthew 6: 6
2. 1 Peter 2: 11
3. 1 Corinthians 2: 14–15
4. *The Ladder of Perfection* by Walter Hilton was a popular devotional work of the time.
5. Matthew 3: 10; Luke 3: 9

FIFTY-FOUR

1. 1 Peter 2: 13
2. 1 Corinthians 10: 33
3. Psalm 29: 2; 96: 7
4. Acts 5: 41
5. Matthew 6: 20
6. Acts 20: 35
7. This may be the origin of the prayer of St Ignatius Loyola including the words: 'To labour and not to ask for any reward save that of knowing that we do Your will.'
8. Matthew 5: 44; Luke 6: 27
9. 1 Corinthians 12: 31
10. Genesis 3: 14–20
11. Ephesians 2: 8
12. Ephesians 1: 14
13. Colossians 3: 10

FIFTY-FIVE

1. Genesis 1: 27
2. Romans 7: 23. The argument of this chapter lies chiefly in Romans 7.
3. Genesis 8: 21
4. Romans 7: 22
5. Romans 7: 12
6. Romans 7: 25
7. Romans 7: 18
8. Philippians 4: 13
9. 1 Corinthians 13: 1–3
10. Psalm 90: 14
11. 2 Corinthians 12: 9
12. Psalm 23: 4
13. Ecclesiasticus 6: 3
14. From an ancient prayer which is used for Trinity 17 in the Book of Common Prayer: 'We pray that Thy grace may always go before and follow us.'

FIFTY-SIX

1. Matthew 9: 9
2. John 14: 6
3. John 8: 32
4. John 8: 12; 1 Timothy 6: 12

5. Matthew 19: 17
6. Matthew 19: 21
7. Matthew 16: 24
8. Matthew 10: 24
9. John 13: 17
10. John 15: 12
11. John 14: 21
12. Revelation 3: 21
13. Hebrews 12: 2
14. 1 Maccabees 3: 59
15. 1 Maccabees 9: 10

FIFTY-SEVEN

1. Isaiah 49: 18
2. Baruch 4: 30
3. This is a reference to the tradition that the Devil was a fallen Angel.
4. Job 5: 11
5. Psalm 19: 10; 119: 103
6. Luke 23: 42

FIFTY-EIGHT

1. Psalm 119: 137
2. Romans 11: 33
3. 2 Timothy 2: 23
4. 1 Corinthians 14: 33
5. Psalm 21: 3
6. Romans 8: 29
7. John 15: 19
8. Galatians 1: 15
9. Matthew 18: 10
10. Wisdom 6: 7
11. John 17: 21
12. Revelation 4: 10
13. Matthew 18: 1
14. Matthew 5: 9
15. Isaiah 60: 22; 65: 20
16. Matthew 18: 3-4
17. Luke 6: 24
18. 2 John 4

FIFTY-NINE

1. Psalm 91: 2
2. Philippians 2: 21
3. Romans 8: 28
4. Psalm 123: 1; 141: 8
5. Psalm 23: 4; Isaiah 9: 2
6. Luke 1: 79

THE STORY OF PENGUIN CLASSICS

Before 1946 ... 'Classics' are mainly the domain of academics and students; readable editions for everyone else are almost unheard of. This all changes when a little-known classicist, E. V. Rieu, presents Penguin founder Allen Lane with the translation of Homer's *Odyssey* that he has been working on in his spare time.

1946 Penguin Classics debuts with *The Odyssey*, which promptly sells three million copies. Suddenly, classics are no longer for the privileged few.

1950s Rieu, now series editor, turns to professional writers for the best modern, readable translations, including Dorothy L. Sayers's *Inferno* and Robert Graves's unexpurgated *Twelve Caesars*.

1960s The Classics are given the distinctive black covers that have remained a constant throughout the life of the series. Rieu retires in 1964, hailing the Penguin Classics list as 'the greatest educative force of the twentieth century.'

1970s A new generation of translators swells the Penguin Classics ranks, introducing readers of English to classics of world literature from more than twenty languages. The list grows to encompass more history, philosophy, science, religion and politics.

1980s The Penguin American Library launches with titles such as *Uncle Tom's Cabin*, and joins forces with Penguin Classics to provide the most comprehensive library of world literature available from any paperback publisher.

1990s The launch of Penguin Audiobooks brings the classics to a listening audience for the first time, and in 1999 the worldwide launch of the Penguin Classics website extends their reach to the global online community.

The 21st Century Penguin Classics are completely redesigned for the first time in nearly twenty years. This world-famous series now consists of more than 1300 titles, making the widest range of the best books ever written available to millions – and constantly redefining what makes a 'classic'.

The Odyssey continues ...

The best books ever written

PENGUIN 🐧 CLASSICS

SINCE 1946

Find out more at www.penguinclassics.com